Teaching Critical Thinking

Philosophy of Education Research Library

Series editors
  V. A. Howard and Israel Scheffler
  Harvard Graduate School of Education

Recent decades have witnessed the decline of distinctively philosophical thinking about education. Practitioners and the public alike have increasingly turned rather to psychology, the social sciences and to technology in search of basic knowledge and direction. However, philosophical problems continue to surface at the center of educational concerns, confronting educators and citizens as well with inescapable questions of value, meaning, purpose, and justification.

PERL will publish works addressed to teachers, school administrators and researchers in every branch of education, as well as to philosophers and the reflective public. The series will illuminate the philosophical and historical bases of educational practice, and assess new educational trends as they emerge.

Already published

The Uses of Schooling
  Harry S. Broudy

Educating Reason: Rationality, Critical Thinking and Education
  Harvey Siegel

Thinking in School and Society
  Francis Schrag

Plato's Metaphysics of Education
  Samuel Scolnicov

The Sense of Art: A Study in Aesthetic Education
  Ralph A. Smith

The Teacher: Theory and Practice in Education
  Allen Pearson

Liberal Justice and the Marxist Critique of Education
  Kenneth A. Strike

Philosophical Foundations of Health Education
  Ronald S. Laura and Sandra Heaney

Varieties of Thinking
  V. A. Howard

Accountability in Education: A Philosophical Inquiry
  Robert B. Wagner

Teaching Critical Thinking

Dialogue and Dialectic

John E. McPeck

Foreword by Michael Scriven

Routledge

New York   London

Published in 1990 by

Routledge
An imprint of Routledge, Chapman and Hall, Inc.
29 West 35 Street
New York, NY 1001

Published in Great Britain by

Routledge
11 New Fetter Lane
London EC4P 4EE

Library of Congress Cataloging in Publication Data

McPeck, John E.
    Teaching critical thinking / John E. McPeck.
        p. cm.—(Philosophy of education research library)
    ISBN 0-415-90225-8
    1. Education—Philosophy. 2. Critical thinking—Study and
teaching. 3. McPeck, John E. I. Title. II. Series.
LB885.M35T43 1990
370.15′2—dc20   89-29791

British Library Cataloguing in Publication Data also available.

*This book is dedicated to my
friend James T. Sanders*

Contents

Foreword

If the critical thinking movement can't look critically at itself, it does not deserve to graduate into the curriculum. The best gymnastics coach in the world is an incompetent gymnast—to be precise, he is a shotputter who married a gymnast—and there's no reason to think he'd be any better as a coach if he were a better gymnast. He might be worse. But it's different with critical thinking. "Do as I say, not as I do" can sometimes save an individual, but it can't save a movement or a political party. And the nearer the individual is to being a preacher, the harder it is to get away with this excuse, on the airwaves or in the classroom. Even doctors who smoke lose credibility.

Well, the critical thinking movement is not too far from being a band of preachers, preachers about the normative economy of reasoning. John McPeck is the bookkeeper, the man who comes around to remind us of what we owe, according to the principles of our own sermons. In fact, he comes around with a large bill already made out. We have all benefited from struggling to decide whether we owe that much to reason. In the end, he has at least forced us to restructure our sermons substantially.

Most academic subjects have fallen victim to the Sirens of the ivory tower—sacrificing utility in favor of elegant abstraction, to various degrees at various times in their history. Perhaps economics and philosophy have the worst record of all, a short head in front of psychology. Modern academic logic, until the informal logic movement got rolling, was another of the worst offenders, despite its claims of clarification. The irony of McPeck's challenge is the suggestion that our mighty multitextual body of practical advice and maxims is just another masquerade, a spirit that wears a mask of practicality but in reality has no more practical content than *Principia Mathematica*—except when it steals it from some respectable empirical subject.

I think there is an answer to his challenge, in terms of a three-planked platform that can be trodden without violating his strictures. It may be of some interest to set the answer I propose against the somewhat grander ones more fully defended in this book, especially since I think McPeck implicitly accepts this answer, that is, his practice illustrates it admirably.

Our tasks, it seems to me, are: (i) to teach students how to use the English language's vast repertoire of logical terms (including the exlegal terms like *prima facie* that refer to reasoning, and the marginally scientific terms like *necessary condition*), which they can use to improve their analysis of and communication about argument and presentation; (ii) to provide them with some simple devices and refinements of that vocabulary, which further facilitate logical analysis—tree structures and Venn diagrams, the occasional useful label for a fallacy or a logical distinction (such as the distinction between cause and reason); and (iii) to bring all this to bear, not only on a thousand everyday examples, but on some of the great nonsubjects of our time, the concepts and topics—and practices—that have not yet become an official part of the general curriculum, but which demand the most rigorous intellectual consideration by every citizen. One can select from such notions as addiction and preventive war, ageism, suicide by terminally ill AIDS victims, brainwashing, the decision-theoretic and other assumptions behind the use (or banning) of nuclear power plants, unconscious corruption of the press, carnivorism, the relevance of the sex life of candidates to their candidacy, causes vs. reasons for the death penalty, or any of a hundred more.

Each of these examples we use—the simple practical ones and the mighty issues—is "about some specific subject or thing," in McPeck's terms. So we agree with him there. Using the English vocabulary of reason, we can make important points about each topic, as he does about his critics in this book. We, like he, are then applying the general distinctions and metalanguage of argument and presentation which I suggest constitutes the specific subject matter of information logic. Yet we can agree with him that there is no great new subject matter of logic, for this is simply the vocabulary of the careful user of the native tongue; the "logic in language" rather than the "language of logic."

There will of course be no time in a critical thinking course, nor the expertise, to cover all of the content related to these issues. But some most important points of a logical kind can be made about many of the arguments and feelings stirred up by these issues. The notion of, and some skills in, reasoning as a crucial clarification process can thus be taught without the need for delving into vast subject matters; and without the claim that some large and separate subject matter of its own is being brought to bear.

Although it seems at times that he is denying its possibility, McPeck himself does exactly this kind of analysis in this book— that is, analysis that depends on refined use of the vocabulary of reasoning without deep entry into substantive subject matter. (For example, he plausibly criticizes Norris for confusing causal questions with questions of meaning.) His ability to do that is an example of his application of his own reasoning skill, in terms of my simple geography of such things. What he does can surely be extended to a myriad other cases without running into the need for greater subject matter excursions or more general skills—and what he does, or something that approximates to it, can be taught. The difference between the pre-test and post-test scores on a critical thinking test that has been purged of vocabulary dependence are, in my experience, very substantial.

"Reasoning ability" is, operationally and pedagogically, a finite set of skills in using a finite box of tools, and we should leave to the psychologists the question whether a general factor loads the test performances. The term *handyman* covers a similarly wide range of skills, and we have no hesitation in using it when deserved, despite the huge differences between the skills of measuring, planing, painting, and tracing circuits or fixing taps.

Here, McPeck threatens us with the other horn of the dilemma. On this approach, he warns, we will run into an impossible task because of the colossal number of critical thinking skills we would have to cover. Of course, we can easily develop critical thinking inventories of enormous size, just as tool fiends enrich their workshops with fifty different screwdrivers and forty files—and not without reason. But there is no *strong* need for all that; one big Swiss Army knife can be provided and mastered in an introductory course and will serve our students very well in solving many, many problems. Is that really true? Ask yourself how many logical terms you actually use in dealing with the next twenty problems to which you apply critical thinking skills. Try it with the item pool for your course in critical thinking, or with a random sample of items from a text you like; or on the letters to the editor across a week's reading of papers and magazines. It's surprising if you need more than ten. And the twenty after that may need only one more. The curve flattens fast. Check it out. The Swiss Army knife is extremely useful; and affordable in the economy of the curriculum.

Perhaps now the three-pronged pedagogical task outlined above will seem too modest an enterprise to many. Consider it carefully. It is by no means trivial. I suggest the task is large enough, important enough, and interesting enough to keep us busy without busywork. Grander programs seem to me to run onto the horns of McPeck's many dilemmas. This book is an excellent guide to the sharpness and location of those horns. He is a master of the dilemma. Should we suppose that such mastery is unteachable? Surely not; but then, if teachable, surely it is a paradigm of reasoning skill?

Michael Scriven

Preface

In 1979–80, when I was writing *Critical Thinking and Education,* there were relatively few school programs specifically designed to teach critical thinking as such, and even fewer theoretical analyses of the concept "critical thinking." At that time, I had to search disparate sources to find any sustained published discussions of critical thinking. If one were to undertake that same task today, he or she would face the opposite problem from the one I had then. Now one could almost say, without being too cynical, that there is too much material being published on critical thinking in education. Critical thinking programs have proliferated far beyond anything one could have expected in 1979. Not surprisingly, the preponderance of this material is practical, hands-on, "how-to-do-it" texts and workbooks. Seldom does this material directly raise any of the deeper and more controversial questions about what "critical thinking" actually means, what it logically entails, or whether or not its putative "skills" are in fact *generalizable* (and if generalizable, in what sense). Most of these fundamental questions remain moot. And it is these fundamental questions about critical thinking which the present volume attempts to address. Therefore, this is not another practical textbook in the sense that it promises to teach you how to *do* anything. Rather, it seeks to broaden our perspective about critical thinking texts which do make such promises.

This collection of essays grew alongside of (if not *out* of) the proliferation of literature on critical thinking which has been taking place since 1981. This book is a response to that literature of praxis in the sense that it tries to lay bare some of the questionable assumptions which permeate its prescriptions and programs. The point of this challenge is not so much to gain converts to the views contained here, but rather, it is an attempt to bring into the forefront certain questions about critical thinking which I believe are more fundamental than, and have primacy over, the more practical problems of implementation. Certain crucial questions always take precedence over implementation decisions. With critical thinking programs, like nuclear power stations, we are well advised to consider the *need* for and *desirability* of them, before we decide on the type and where to put it.

Each essay in part I is complete and independent of the others; so they may be read alone or in the order presented. However, the arguments in each of these essays are pieces, or subplots, of a more general point of view about critical thinking. That general view is, briefly, that specific subject content determines the required ingredients for thinking critically in each case. One of the more unwelcome consequences of this view is that the notion of "general critical thinking skills" is largely meaningless. Therefore, the great bulk of critical thinking programs which exist today are seriously misguided, in my view.

The essays in part II comprise an interesting (I hope) dialectic between my view and the views of Stephen Norris, Harvey Siegel, and Richard Paul, all of whom take serious exception to my opinions, either in part or in whole. The critiques offered by Norris, Siegel, and Paul are independently worthwhile, because they raise the right questions and pose plausible solutions to them. These essays help to raise the dialectic about critical thinking to a level of debate where I think serious educators should be most concerned. That, alas, is the point of this entire collection. Without at least some heat, there can be no light.

A final word about the origin and chronology of these essays. As mentioned, each paper was originally written as a response to developments which took place in the field of critical thinking during the years 1982–86. With the exception of essays 3 and 4, the essays were written in the order that they are presented here. Essays 3 and 4 were written explicitly for this volume, and have been inserted where they are simply to provide a more natural development of the overall position being presented. My response to Norris and Siegel is a combined and greatly expanded version of what originally appeared in publication. In reading these essays one will note references to my earlier book *Critical Thinking and Education;* however, direct acquaintance with that book is unnecessary. The reader of these essays will recognize the same general point of view being more specifically developed in the issues treated by part I of this volume. It is my hope, and intent, that these essays might stand by themselves as a contribution to some of the unresolved questions generated by the critical thinking movement.

I would particularly like to thank Stephen Norris, Harvey Siegel, and Richard Paul, not only for their generosity in making this book possible, but especially for the quality and sincerity of effort represented by each of their papers. As the dust starts to settle, it appears that some of their arrows may be on target, and I think we are all better off for it.

Acknowledgments

I gratefully acknowledge the following publishers for allowing me to reprint versions of papers which originally appeared as copyright material: *Canadian Journal of Education* 9:1 (1984), "Stalking Beasts but Swatting Flies: The Teaching of Critical Thinking"; *Teaching Philosophy* 8:4 (October 1985), "Critical Thinking and the 'Trivial Pursuit' Theory of Knowledge"; *Informal Logic* 4:2 (July 1984), "The Evaluation of Critical Thinking Programs"; also *Informal Logic* 7:1 (Winter 1985), "McPeck's Mistakes," by Richard Paul, and my response, "Paul's Critique." I would also like to thank the Philosophy of Education Society for allowing me to reproduce the exchange of papers which took place between Stephen P. Norris, Harvey Siegel, and myself at the Fifth General Session of their 1985 meetings in New Orleans (Published as *Proceedings of the Phil. of Educ. Soc. 1985*).

Teaching Critical Thinking

PART I

The position

CHAPTER 1

What kind of knowledge will transfer?

Every book or paper I have ever read, and every person I have ever asked, claims that the purpose of critical thinking is, in one way or another, to improve people's reasoning ability about everyday problems and issues. This aim, indeed, would appear to be straightforward enough and given the complex world we live in, few educational goals could be more laudable. But as simple and straightforward as this goal is to state, there is an important confusion over what it means. In particular, the basic notions of "reasoning ability" and "everyday problems" admit of more than one interpretation. And how one interprets these notions determines in large measure the type of instruction one designs to promote critical thinking. I, for one, continue to be surprised at how much more the standard approaches to critical thinking seem designed to fit the ready-made solutions than the solutions are made to fit the problem.

The standard approaches to critical thinking (this would include the work of Robert Ennis, Howard Kahane, Johnson and Blair, and Scriven's book *Reasoning*) all reduce the notions of "reasoning ability" and "everyday problem" to what have come to be called "argument analysis" or "everyday argument." More often than not they go on to collapse these distinctions by simply talking about "everyday reasoning"—a phrase which has a nice ring about it if for no other reason than it suggests something which is clear and understood by everybody. And on the face of it, what could be more useful? Thus, it is not surprising that students should flock to courses in critical thinking or informal logic after reading the enticing promissory notes contained in course descriptions. Indeed, there is a burgeoning cottage industry in textbooks and materials promising to improve everyday reasoning—as though this merely required a few special methods and skills. I suspect, in fact, that "argument analysis" has just the right amount of technical connotation, mixed with an intriguing jargon, to lend it the required air of legitimacy for commercial appeal. Perish the thought, but perhaps we are not far from the radio call-in show offering psychological help and counseling to all who would avail themselves. Unwittingly no doubt, but courses entitled "Speed Reasoning," and the like, come dangerously close to this kind of merchandising.

To underscore this trend, notice how far we have come: from the longstanding and legitimate need to improve reasoning about complex social problems o the quick-fix course in "everyday reasoning" and "argument analysis." Surely things cannot be so simple. We have not, to my knowledge, recently discovered any new miracle cure for the longstanding frailty of human judgment. Not one nor even three courses in critical thinking are likely to overcome this known deficiency in the educational process. Where did we go wrong? What accounts for the boundless enthusiasm for critical thinking courses as the hope for the future? Have we begun to believe our own promotional literature and taken its claims too seriously?

Reasoning ability

As noted, the standard approaches to critical thinking tend to fuse the notions of "reasoning ability," "argument analysis," and "everyday reasoning," using these terms almost interchangeably and treating them as one homogeneous ball of wax. But it is precisely at this point where we begin to go wrong; and this partially explains why we have been duped into taking our own rhetoric more seriously than performance justifies.

To take them one at a time, the notion of "reasoning ability" introduces several dificulties which quickly get lost in the shuffle. Notice that even to use a phrase like "reasoning ability" suggests that we are dealing with a single underlying capability. That is, we use "reasoning ability" in much the same way that we refer to the ability to speak English, say— either one does or does not possess the skill. For example, statements like "Ronald Reagan *does,* but Aleksey Kosygin *does not* speak English" accentuate this binary conception of language skill. Despite the fact that we can (and do) speak of a person using English more or less well, we still tend to think of it as an either/or skill. But what leads us to think that reasoning ability similarly denotes a singular skill? It could be that we have been led astray by the grammar of the phrase, thinking (uncritically!) that it too must denote some ontological reality. (Gilbert Ryle, where are you?!) Whatever the reason for such beguiling usage, reasoning ability covers all manner of cognitive phenomena, scarcely any cluster of which resembles another. Just as chess and crossword puzzles require reasoning ability, so does finding one's way home, investing money, fishing, driving a car, doing sums, shopping, playing hopscotch, voting intelligently, building math models, writing poems, and countless other classes of activities. Thus, the phrase "reasoning ability" does not denote any particular skill, nor indeed any particular *kind* of skill. About all that these activities have in common is that they are all done by conscious beings and require reasoning of some sort.

Elsewhere I have suggested that the concept of reasoning ability functions something like the concept of "speed" (see my *Critical Thinking and Educational* 1981). If, out of the blue, someone offered to improve our *speed,* the first thing we would properly ask is, "At what?" We'd probably all like to be speedier at running, or reading, or typing, or even changing mufflers, but we know that no single course could improve our speed at all things. Given that the range of things over which we'd like to improve our "reasoning ability" is perhaps even wider than the range of activities in which we might desire to improve our speed, then the prospects for improving our general reasoning ability are even dimmer. And the reason they are dim, I'm suggesting, is that the very notion of "general reasoning ability" is, upon reflection, incoherent.[1] At the very least, clarity will be served and progress more likely if we simply drop the phrase "reasoning ability" from our critical thinking lexicon. to be honest, and clear, we are not in the business of improving reasoning ability *simpliciter.*

Argument analysis

When the literature in informal logic and critical thinking uses the phrase "reasoning ability," is is usually referring to the reasoning involved in argument analysis. Indeed "reasoning ability" and "argument analysis" are sometimes used interchangeably. Again, however, these two notions are hardly equivalent.[2] In fact, I would argue that "argument analysis," as such, comprises only a very small portion of reasoning ability. In the early pages of *Reasoning* (p. 7), Scriven points out that there is no *a priori* reason to believe that animals do not reason, since some clearly manifest behavior which should count as reasoning. I have no quarrel with this observation, but surely he does not mean that they reason in the sense that they analyze arguments. Argument analysis, after all, has to do with the assessment of relations between propositions, and not only do animals not do this, but they would have little use for it if they did. I am sufficiently confident in saying this about animals because I'm convinced that the value of argument analysis has been greatly oversold to humans.

If one could calmly and objectively determine how much of an intelligent person's reasoning is actually spent analyzing arguments as such, I would be surprised if it reached 5 percent. (My social-science friends, by the way, are always dazzled by the statistical rigor with which I arrive at such figures!) In reasoning our way through the day, the month, or even the year, the bulk of our mental effort is spent choosing and deciding, solving problems, learning *how to do* things, interpreting meanings (e.g., complex statements or concepts, train schedules, tax laws, etc.), and perhaps most importantly, determining the *truth,* not the validity, of various statements and putative evidence. Argument analysis, on the other hand, as we have come to know it, is quite beside the major point of such reasoning. While it is true that argment analysis can something play a role in some (though not all) of these reasoning tasks, it is of limited value because: (1) argument analysis is always an *ex post facto* reconstruction of past reasoning, positing neither alternatives nor hypotheses for future consideration; and (2) the major focus of argument analysis is to determine the validity of arguments, not the truth of premises or evidence. And the truth (of premises) is more difficult to determine, but unquestionably of more value in practical affairs.

When one stops to think about it, the differentiation of validity from invalidity, as such, is a nearly exclusive preoccupation of logicians—and a fairly specialized or esoteric preoccupation at that. But when nonlogicians (e.g., business executives, artists, or average citizens) express an interest in improving their reasoning ability, I doubt that the systematic study of validity or soundness of arguments is what they have in mind. And as interesting a pursuit as argument analysis is, it remains little more than an article of faith that it provides the kind of reasoning improvement required for our complex social world. Moreover, this is as true of informal logical analysis as it is of the deductive variety. I agree with the view that effective reasoning is perhaps more important now than it ever was; but the study of argument analysis, formal or informal, seems an unlikely means for achieving that goal. As a philosopher, I have as much respect and appreciation for argument analysis as anyone, and I am aware of its obvious utility. But I do not think we are doing anyone a service by regarding it as the equivalent to, or a substitute for, general reasoning ability.

By liberally reinterpreting the general problems demanding reasoning, we have twisted the problem to fit our ready-made and cherished solutions—informal logic and argument analysis. We have mistaken the most visible tip of the iceberg (i.e., argument analysis) for the entire object. On the rare occasion when this view of reasoning is seriously questioned, we comfort ourselves with accepting the answer, "Oh well, even if argument analysis isn't the whole of reasoning, it's clearly the most important part of it." I think a more likely conclusion would be, "Since argument analysis is the only way that we philosophers know to describe reasoning, it must be synonymous with reasoning itself."

Everyday argument

In addition to the notions of reasoning ability and argument analysis, yet another troublesome term remains which requires scrutiny. That is the recurrent notion of "everyday argument," which is meant to circumscribe the domain of informal logic. Johnson and Blair suggest (perhaps correctly) that the phrase is meant to cover all those arguments which we might think of as "practical," "everyday," "ordinary," and/or "mundane," as distinct from "formal" or "mathematical" arguments. Perhaps the longer phrase "ordinary everyday arguments" captures this domain best. Be that as it may, the literature and textbooks on informal logic nevertheless gloss over and abuse this notion more than any other idea or concept in the area. Indeed, a much-needed paper still waits to be written on the concept of "everyday argument" and all that the phrase entails.

For the present, however, let us set aside the definitional question, simply accept Johnson and Blair's characterization of "everyday argument," and begin to consider what has to be known in order to analyze an everyday argument. That is, let us focus more closely on the actual ingredients of an everyday argument. As we proceed, we should bear in mind that the truth of the premises is every bit as important as the validity of the argument. This point is worth repeating not only because the analysis of real argument requires it, but also because informal logic distinguishes itself from formal logic in its preemptive concern with *soundness* in contrast to simple *validity*. Let us further agree (with the standard approach) that everyday argument is typically concerned with public issues of the sort that informed citizens must decide upon. Recent examples of such issues might include Reagan's economic policies, American intervention in El Salvador, economic sanctions against Poland, creationism versus evolution in science classes, nuclear disarmament, minority and women's rights, gun control, plea bargaining, nuclear power stations, etc. Several things can safely be observed about such issues. First, the survival of a healthy democracy requires public debate about such questions. Second, our public schools would like to prepare people for making intelligent decisions about such questions. Third, these are the sorts of questions where honest and intelligent disagreement is possible, even likely. Finally, these are complex issues in the sense that they typically encompass a substantial amount of information or putative facts, some of which are likely to be independently contentious.

Now the standard formal logic approach to such issues is to take an existing argument and examine it for any fallacies, formal or informal, that might affect its validity. This, in fact, is the strongest suit of the standard approach. Failing that, or when fallacies are not found, then the standard approach suggests looking for unstated assumptions and/or questioning the truth of given premises. If fault can be found in any of these facets of the argument, the one has objective grounds for rejecting the argument. This, admittedly, is a thumbnail sketch of the procedure, but a reasonably faithful characterization of the overall strategy.

Several serious shortcomings of this strategy deserve attention. Notice first that even if a *bona fide* fallacy is discovered in a given argument, one still cannot infer from this that the opposite point of view is correct. To so infer would be a clear case of "affirming the consequent." At best, all that one can infer is that *this* particular argument is fallacious, but for all that the general point of view could still be true (or preferable). Therefore, in this type of public issue, one is still not able to make an intelligent decision on the question simply because he or she knows that a particular argument is fallacious. Thus, detecting fallacies is not as useful (or practical) to the decision maker as some might assume. One still does not know what is right, true, or correct. I do no mean to suggest that validity, as such, is irrelevant to weighty public issues, but merely that its usefulness is quite limited in deciding such questions.

With respect to that phase of argument analysis called "assumption hunting," proponents of informal logic are already painfully aware of the difficulties inherent in this task. I do not, therefore, want to dwell on these problems here beyond making two points which have not received sufficient attention. First, it should be recognized that by making suitable assumptions it is always possible, in principle at least, to make a given argument as strong (or as weak) as one wants. For example, if the "principle of charity" is taken far enough one could take any abysmally weak argument and nurse it back to health: it simply requires positing suitable assumptions for it. Conversely, practical syllogisms which are otherwise strong can be weakened if suitable contexts, conditions or assumptions are brought to bear on them. What is to be regarded as "suitable" in either case will be determined by contingent contexts, beliefs, values, and judgments, etc., which perforce go beyond any set of rules, formal or informal. This is because rational judgment is distilled from a matrix of values and beliefs with infinite combinations.

The second point about looking for "unstated assumptions" is that when a single argument is being examined, such as one finds on an editorial page, there is no method for determining what assumptions the author might actually be making. And short of being psychic, there can be no such method. This is because there is potentially an indeterminate number of possible assumptions underlying any given premise. Moreover, each of these possible assumptions may have an indeterminate number of assumptions underlying them. The various suggestions we have seen in the literature, from Scriven and others, for avoiding a "straw-man," using the "principle of charity," and making "minimal assumptions" are all designed to create assumptions about the argument. I wish to stress the point that these new assumptions are created for the argument, rather than found or discovered, as the phrase "assumption hunting" might suggest. As "unstated assumptions," they do not come as part of the original argument. The analyst simply infers certain assumptions, even though they are not necessarily implied by the argument. When one does this, however, one is no longer analyzing the actual argument given but an altered or preferred interpretation of it. And this, I would suggest, is a very dangerous business indeed, not only because it can easily strap someone with an assumption that they were not in fact making, but also because it threatens to strip argument analysis of its objective integrity by encouraging subjective interpretations.

Clearly, something is wrong in this business of "assumption hunting," and that is the belief that assumption hunting is necessary for argument analysis. I submit that assumption hunting is neither necessary nor desirable in argument analysis. It is undesirable for the reasons suggested above. The only reason assumption hunting might appear necessary in the first place rests on confusing an *assumption* with a *presupposition*. But these are both logically and psychologically distinct. To wit: an assumption of an argument can be false yet the argument itself remain sound. By contrast, if a presupposition of an argument is false, then the argument cannot be sound.[3] Assumptions, after all, have more to do with the contingent belief state of the arguer than with the objective validity of an argument. So, unless we are more interested in showing that some individual happens to be making a mistake (as one might in a debating society), we would be better advised to seek out false presuppositions, and treat assumption hunting as largely beside the point.

This whole tactic of assumption hunting points to the larger question of the ultimate purpose of argument analysis and critical thinking. Is the purpose essentially to refine disputation, or to pursue truth through rational inquiry? If its purpose is disputation, then it is difficult to see how this differs from classical rhetoric, where "winning" takes precedence over knowledge and truth; and it is similarly difficult to believe that schools and colleges intend argument analysis for this purpose. If, on the other hand, its purpose is to pursue truth, as I think it should be, then the emphasis upon "everyday argument" not only creates the wrong impression about its purpose (suggesting rhetoric and disputation), but it seriously restricts its potential for finding truth. For the complex issues which generate public argument, and where rational disagreement is possible, truth is more evasive than the simple tools of everyday argument imply. Emphasizing everyday argument, as such, yields little more than "everyday" solutions, the reason being that the tools suited for everyday argument (e.g., informal logic, etc.) are no match for the complexities of everyday controversial issues.

By the phrase "everyday argument," no one, to my knowledge, means the kind of argument we might have about whose turn it is to walk the dog after dinner, or whether the family garden is going to need two rows of carrots this year, or whether the new weatherman represents an improvement over the old. Rather, we are all, philosophers and educators alike, concerned about those public issues that might seriously affect the well-being of society in some way. And these public issues move us into the arena of complex information where the lion's share of the difficulty comes from the intelligibility and reliability of this information. The major deficiency, as I see it, with the standard treatments of everyday argument is that they depreciate the important and complex role of information by positing an equivalence between "everyday argument" and "everyday problems." However, everyday argument is no match for the complexities of everyday problems. Thus, even where the standard approaches to everyday argument purport to be at their best, namely in the context of "everyday problems," they fall far short in their own chosen domain. To appreciate this, let's look at some everyday problems.

Everyday problems

Typical classroom examples of everyday problems are taken from various public sources such as printed speeches, editorials, or media accounts of various social issues. Arguments either for or against something are singled out and then examined for their validity and soundness. The techniques, strategies, and rules of formal and informal logic are the major tools employed to perform these analyses; and students are taught to become proficient in the use of these tools through drills, practice, and discussion. However, I contend that this approach to everyday problems is largely a waste of time, money, and effort, because the real difficulty in assessing these questions has little to do with fallacies and validity, and almost everything to do with understanding complex information.[4] In the language of informal logic, the problem is not with establishing *validity* but of establishing *soundness:* the soundness (i.e., truth) of both individual premises and entire arguments.

One need look no further than the nearest newspaper or television to find typical issues. For example, in his State of the Union Address, President Reagan defended his economic policies by claiming that "inflation is coming down and things are getting better. And if we simply stay on this track things will continue to improve." This at least was the gist of his position, and so far as it went it sounded coherent and plausible. Inflation, after all, is not easy to lick, and West Germany and Japan had to bite the bullet for five years to bring theirs under control. However, immediately following Reagan's speech, the Democrats spelled out the adverse effects of Reagan's economic policies. They pointed out that unemployment, bankruptcies, and interest rates were at record highs, and that all of their indicators suggested, contrary to Reagan's claims, that things would continue to get worse.

I listened carefully to both presentations, and afterwards to several commentaries and heated journalistic exchanges. What struck me about this "everyday problem" was that there were no obvious "fallacies" committed in either presentation. Indeed, both sides seemed to build a reasonable case. Since I could detect no fallacies, my years of teaching logic, both formal and informal, were of discouragingly little use to me. What I needed to know was whether the various premises offered were in fact true. In subsequent days, as I sought out the truth of these premises, I found myself immersed in Laffer curves, zero-sum systems, monetary versus fiscal policies, and various other concepts and propositions which I was not sure I could even understand, much less determine whether they were in fact true. In short, what I needed to know was more economics, not more logic. This problem, let us not forget, is one of those typical garden-variety, common, mundane, "everyday" problems which average citizens commonly discuss, argue about, and often vote upon. It is precisely in dealing with this kind of problem where the standard approach to informal logic and critical thinking *purports* to be most useful. Indeed, the standard approach to critical thinking justifies its existence on the grounds that it enables people to make more rational judgments about "everyday problems" of just this sort. However, the reason that the standard approach cannot deliver what it advertises is that it can only examine and pass on *validity* relationships, and is ill equipped to determine *truth*. But in most everyday problems worthy of public debate our quandary is seldom about validity, and almost always about the truth of complex information, concepts, and propositions (such as the example above). We are not analyzing arguments so much as evaluating data, information, and putative facts.

This observation is quite general. One could pick virtually any "everyday problem" and find oneself falling into similar quandaries. For example, the nuclear disarmament debate quickly brings one into the technical arena of ICBMs, MERVs, cruise missiles, MXs, first-strike capabilities, deterrence, so-called windows of vulnerability, zero options, and many other complex considerations which might make a significant difference on precisely whether or how disarmament should proceed. Also in foreign and defense policy, most decisions that a society must make are between what appears *undesirable* and what is *unacceptable,* and before understanding which is which, you usually have to possess a lot of information and accept certain judgments of prognostication. In the end, either choice is awkward and unpleasant since there are few pure and untainted decisions in such matters. Even the "everyday problems" closer to home, such as the rights of minorities, affirmative action, nuclear power plants, tax roll-back proposals such as California's Proposition 13, product safety, and the like require being in possession of, and comprehending, large amounts of complex information. There simply is no short-cut around this brute fact about the complexities of what are misleadingly called "everyday problems." Moreover, 98 percent of our mistakes (note: my dazzling statistics again!) in rational judgment originate in this informational domain, either because we don't have enough of it, or because our sources are unreliable, or as often as not because we do not understand the empirical foundations and meaning of the information we do have.

At my university, for example, the Department of Budget and Finance has created, of necessity, a new sub-branch called the "Information Analysis Office." Its purpose is to assist university financial specialists in understanding the implications and significance of their own data. It is clear to me that if we are serious about getting at the *truth* of a particular "everyday problem," we would be similarly well advised to spend most of our effort on "information analysis." But in doing this, we move directly into specific domains of expertise, or what Kenneth Strike has called "specialists' guilds."

This suggestion is anathema to proponents of the standard approach to everyday argument since the standard approach attempts to bypass these problems by assuming that the requisite information is usually "common knowledge." But when and if the requisite information is in fact "common knowledge," then I would argue that "common sense" can handle it— indeed, this is what "common sense" means. However, the point I have been trying to make is that the type of social problem we are all concerned about in everyday argument is nearly always complicated, and the reason it is complicated is because the requisite information is. As was suggested earlier, the very notions of "everyday argument" and "everyday problem" are not at all clear, because when you get close to them there is nothing particularly mundane, ordinary, or simple about them. That is why such problems keep reappearing *every day*.

It seems to me that the major flaw in the standard approach to everyday argument is its tendency to make what is in fact complex seem relatively simple and straightforward. Indeed, there is an interesting parallel here with certain tendencies of television news broadcasting. Many critics of television news have pointed out the sundry ways that the medium can be used to distort or manipulate public opinion. How, for example, it tends to reflect the biases of the press corps at times, and in turn how this tends to increase with the importance of the events in question. Still others have pointed out how stories with flashy visuals command more coverage than stories with less of a visual dimension, even though these latter stories might be more important. Whatever the truth of these various criticisms, a still more insidious effect of television news is worth considering—the fact that viewers typically get their knowledge and opinions of complex human events from three-minute "spots" on television. It is as though "everyday reality" comes packaged in three-minute bits, and anything beyond that is either esoteric or not particularly significant. We have become quite used to boiled down versions of truth, as though you might come to know the real Joe DiMaggio from information provided on bubblegum cards. This is a dangerous trend that fosters superficiality. And insofar as the standard approach to critical thinking typically reduces the necessary information to "common knowledge," as though this is all that is required, it tends to foster the same kind of superficiality. The result is a caricature of critical thinking, not the genuine item.

General skills for critical thinking

So far, one might well get the impression that I believe the standard approach to critical thinking (like pornography) has no redeeming social value. This is not the case. The standard academic discipline can profit considerably from much of the material in critical thinking courses. And conversely, the standard approach to critical thinking has at least as much to gain from the traditional academic disciplines—perhaps more. It might be fair to say that my disagreement with the standard approach to critical thinking is largely pedagogic in character, but this difference, I contend, is significant.

The general rationale which lends plausibility to the standard approach is straightforward enough. Since no one is capable of knowing everything about everything, and because we cannot predict what kinds of knowledge one might require for specific problems in the future, the standard approach chooses to teach certain general principles which apply to all (or most) areas of human knowledge. An impressive economy of effort would seem to be gained if mastery of these general principles can be accomplished, since they apply to almost all problem areas. The standard approach assumes these principles to be those of applied logic, both formal and informal.[5] Thus, the strategy is to maximize transfer by providing students with the general skills for using these logical principles whenever they are needed.

This strategy obviously contrasts with any approach which attempts to teach specific knowledge and information from established fields in that knowledge and information do not, supposedly, transfer beyond their own narrow problem areas. In short, from the "critical thinking" point of view there are two separate arguments against a "knowledge and information" approach. First, knowledge and information lack the transfer potential of general skills. Second, one cannot predict what knowledge and information an individual may need for the future. The general skills of critical thinking, then, are seen to *maximize transfer,* while a "knowledge and information" approach is viewed as "minimizing" transfer. The standard approach views these transfer relationships as shown in figure 1.

This view is indeed plausible, and no doubt accounts for much of the widespread acceptance of the standard approach to critical thinking. There is, in fact, *a kind* of "transfer" that takes place between the critical thinking skills and multiple problem areas. However, I think it important to take a close look at the different senses in which transfer does and does not occur in this view of things, because if my suspicions are correct, the sense in which these skills apply to multiple-problem domains would still not support them (or argue for them) as a means for promoting critical thinking in our schools.

The major point of mastering the general principles of applied logic, or argument analysis, is to maximize the number of problem areas in which a person can be rationally competent. This goal of maximization, however, is both the major appeal and the major weakness of these general skills. Often, as decision theory predicts, when you attempt to maximize one outcome you inevitably minimize another. In this sense, the general skills approach to critical thinking represents a classical tradeoff. In its effort to maximize the number of areas to which its general principles apply, this approach perforce sacrifices genuine effectiveness in all of them. While its prescriptions are generally true, they are also hollow, more truistic, than true—for example: "Make sure the conclusion follows," "Look out for tautologies," "Is a fallacy being committed?" "Don't contradict yourself." Such sage advice resembles a baseball manager exhorting his pitcher to "throw strikes!"

The ineffectiveness of the general skills approach (i.e., applied logic, etc.) to critical thinking is identical to an endemic difficulty in general problem solving from artificial intelligence research. In designing computer programs to solve "ill-structured" or "open-ended" problems, one strategy is to employ certain heuristic devices, or rules of thumb, which will suggest plausible solutions. It is axiomatic, however, that the more general a given heuristic is, the less useful it can be for solving any particular problem. Conversely, the more specific a given heuristic device is, the more likely it is to guarantee solutions for specific problems. Here we have perhaps the paradigmatic tradeoff relationship. Like the general principles of the standard approach, general heuristics are also hollow and virtually useless for specific problems. Such general heuristics as "Seek plausible hypotheses" are the equivalent to urging the pitcher to "throw strikes" and heuristic programers know it. It is time that the so-called general skills of the standard approach were recognized as having the same deficiency, and for the same reasons. Giving people very general principles for solving problems, even with extensive training in them, is like giving people a language with a syntax but no semantic. It is functionally meaningless.

FIGURE 1

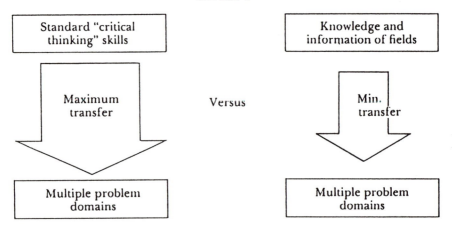

Philosophies-of and critical thinking

What strategy, then, might be more conducive for developing the capacity for critical thinking? It was previously said that there is some merit in the standard approach, but that this material may require a significantly different pedagogical approach. First, I would suggest that we rid ourselves of all talk about "general skills" of critical thinking since it turns out to be a false hope. Second, we need to reconsider the transfer potential of "knowledge and information" to critical thinking. Contrary to the received opinion, it is not at all obvious to me that selected knowledge and information has any less general transfer than the putative skills of the standard approach. Figure 1 presents the standard approach for critical thinking, while figure 2 suggests my own converse hypothesis for critical thinking pedagogy.

I have already argued to the point of tedium that the standard critical thinking skills do not effectively transfer to any significant degree. Specifically, what seems wrong in the standard view is that it confuses the idea of "logical subsumption" with "psychological transfer." That is, while it is quite true that the various logical principles "apply," in some remote sense, to multiple-problem areas, we should not infer from this that psychological transfer must therefore take place between these principles and domains. As Scriven once commented about "new math," one should not confuse the order of logic with the order of pedagogy.

With respect to my hypothesis, *viz.,* that knowledge of fields can transfer to multiple-problem areas, this is true depending on what kind of knowledge one has, and in what fields. Clearly, some kinds of specific knowledge and information will have far more transfer

FIGURE 2

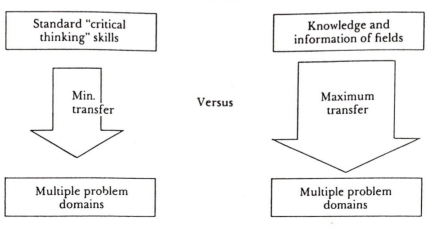

Standard "critical thinking" skills		Knowledge and information of fields
Min. transfer	Versus	Maximum transfer
Multiple problem domains		Multiple problem domains

capacity than other kinds. For example, understanding that "politicians are sensitive to voting pressures" will have far more transfer than understanding "the cat is on the mat." And one can generalize further that certain fields of knowledge will possess more general transfer than others. The problem, then, is not whether specific knowledge and information can transfer, because careful reflection shows that it does, but rather, what knowledge and information will have the most transfer. This question, indeed, is the classical question asked by philosophers of education since the time of Plato, and it remains as crucial today as it did in the past.

From the point of view of developing critical thinkers, my answer to this question has two distinguishable parts. The first concerns the kind of knowledge likely to be the richest or most powerful from the point of view of transfer. The second, of equal importance, concerns the perspective or attitude a person takes with respect to that knowledge. This latter dimension is required of critical thinkers *per se* because it distinguishes the person who merely possesses knowledge, in the sense that he might be trained in it, from the person who reflectively appreciates the strengths and limitations of his own knowledge—if you like, they see it in all of its tentativeness. Rational beliefs as well as rational methods are fallible, after all, and the critical thinker is acutely aware of how and why this is so.

As to the first part of my answer, then, regarding what particular knowledge is the richest and potentially most powerful, my answer may strike some as not sufficiently exciting—such is the grip of our need for novel solutions to old problems. But at the moment, however, I see no competitive substitute for a liberal education. In particular, I am talking about the rational perspective which comes from an informed study of natural and social sciences, together with history, mathematics, literature, and art. We have yet to devise any comparable package which can yield the same breadth of cognitive perspective. Whether by design or by folly, our education system has been more or less on the right track. In its own stumbling, bumbling, bureaucratic way, it may after all be trying to do the right thing. Its failures should not blind us to the potential for success.

This point of view about education is hardly new. I refer you to the work of R. S. Peters, Paul Hirst, and perhaps Jerome Bruner for a sustained defense of it. What I do want to draw your attention to, however, is the second part of my suggestion for developing critical thinkers, because I think it can go some way toward improving upon our past educational efforts while at the same time establishing a crucial role for philosophy to play in this process.

One of the most pervasive shortcomings of the way that the traditional disciplines are taught is that they present their material in such a way that its facts and methods are regarded as nonproblematic. It is as though the foundation of these disciplines was chiseled out of epistemic bedrock, and all one need learn is what the so-called facts are, and how to use its methods for finding more of them. Mastery of these disciplines is too often measured in terms of how many "facts" one has learned, and how proficient one has become in using its "method." Both of these are regarded by teacher and students alike as more or less sacrosanct. The all-too-frequent result of such teaching is that we produce technicians at X and specialists of Y with hardly an educated soul among them. A plausible solution to this problem is to make the philosophy of X and the philosophy of Y an integral part of what it means to "learn X" or to "learn Y." Thus, the philosophy of natural science would be as much a part of science education as Newton's laws. And the insights of the philosophy of history should be as much a part of learning history as the details of the Monroe Doctrine. If I may use a few personal examples, individuals like R. G. Collingwood, Michael Oakeshott, and William Dray might be said to have contributed as much to the study of history as did Samuel Eliot Morrison or Henry Steele Commager. Similar points could be made about the philosophy of art, mathematics, and social science. It should be clear that the philosophy-of approach should not be considered a mere topping-up exercise for the otherwise well-socialized specialist in these disciplines. Rather, the problematic nature of the putative facts and methods of these disciplines should be consciously woven into the fabric of its courses, even at the undergraduate level. In doing so, we would be providing students with the major prerequisites for being critical thinkers.

This is, of course, only a very general outline of the strategy that I would suggest for developing critical thinking capacities. Its three major features are that: (1) it does not presuppose any abstract or general reasoning skills; (2) it employs the power of the disciplines as the chief means for understanding complex concepts and information; and (3) it depends upon the philosophy of these disciplines to provide the required critical dimension to one's understanding.

A more detailed implementation of this proposal would point out the various and sundry ways the philosophy of each discipline could be effectively used to inform the teaching of each discipline. Indeed there are a few (alas too few) works[6] which tacitly employ this strategy already. By contrast to Scriven's book *Reasoning* (1976), these works properly affix critical reasoning to specific kinds of knowledge and information.

One final feature of my proposal is that the standards and rules of logic, both formal and informal, would play a vital role in the philosophy of each discipline. That is, when the philosophy of X is integrated into the subject matter of X, a substantial portion of the philosophic insight would consist in commenting upon and criticizing the patterns of reasoning peculiar to the given discipline. Thus, the tools and rigor of logic are a major bulwark in coming to have a critical understanding of each discipline.

It should be expected, however, that certain types of logic, indeed different insights from logic, will have a greater or lesser role to play depending upon the subject in question. In some instances, formal logic may be virtually irrelevant; in others, understanding certain kinds of fallacies may prove invaluable. But in all instances, the appropriate logic will be a meaningful part of the form of knowledge in question. From this perspective, the use of logic is not an abstract skill, but an integral part of what it means to think rationally in the different fields and disciplines.

It would be fair to say that most of this essay has been spent criticizing the standard approach to critical thinking, especially for not giving due recognition to the complexity and importance of knowledge and information, particularly the knowledge and information derived from the classical disciplines. If space permitted, one could equally show the many ways in which the disciplines could profit from the insights of logicians, both formal and informal. I would like to make it clear, therefore, that I believe the disciplines have as much to learn from the standard approach to critical thinking as the standard approach has to learn from the disciplines. But unless each camp starts taking the other seriously, we will all stalk our respective beasts, but continue to swat flies.

CHAPTER 2

Three competing conceptions of critical thinking

A cousin of mine, who is a businessman, recently asked me what my book on critical thinking has to say about that subject. After I gave him a brief summary of the major thesis of the book, he responded, "You mean to say that you had to write a book to say that? Boy, you academics have a way of making the obvious sound complicated!" Needless to say, I had several qualms about this response. But despite these, I confess to a certain sympathy with it. At times my general view about the nature of critical thinking seems so obvious and commonsensical to me that it is almost embarrassing that it need be said at all, particularly to the learned audience for whom it was originally intended. That audience, incidentally, is what has been called the Informal Logic Movement, which now has an official executive body, a journal, and several annual conferences in the U.S. It includes such familiar textbook authors as Michael Scriven, Robert Ennis, Howard Kahane, Perry Weddle, Walton and Woods, and a growing cadre of informal logic teachers. However, given the discussion (not to mention criticism) which my view has generated within this movement, I am beginning to feel vindicated insofar as what I took to be common sense turns out *not* to be so common at all. There remain some very real differences over what the ingredients of critical thinking are, and how best to teach for it.

The view of critical thinking which I have been defending simply tries to account for certain common, and what I think obvious, facts about human reasoning. At no place does my description of critical thinking appeal to, nor attempt to explain, any mysterious or complex cognitive processes. I would, as it were, be content with a garden-variety account of critical thinking which at least covered the obvious properties of it. I'll leave its more esoteric dimensions for some rainy day.

Here are some of the more obvious points which I attempt to account for. I thought it important to point out that *thinking,* let alone critical thinking, is always about some particular thing or subject (let us call this thing X), and that it therefore makes little or no sense to say, "I

I would like to thank my colleague James T. Sanders for his copious editorial suggestions on an earlier draft of this paper.

teach thinking *simpliciter,*" or "I teach thinking in general but not about anything in particular." All such talk is literal nonsense. (Parenthetically, similar arguments apply to such notions as "creativity" and "problem solving" as well.) No matter how general or abstract the subject matter, if the thinking involved is not about some kind of X, then it is not describable as thinking at all. This consideration, then, binds thinking, and thus critical thinking, to particular subjects or activities. This conclusion represents the first point of departure between my view of critical thinking and what has come to be the standard approach to this subject. Those committed to the standard approach purport to teach courses in critical thinking *simpliciter,* and it doesn't matter what the subject may be about. In my view, this borders on being an absurdity, because there are almost as many ways of thinking as there are things to think about. To claim to teach critical thinking in general, even about mundane "everyday problems," is to make promises which cannot be kept. What is worse, it simply confuses conscientious teachers who are trying to improve the various thinking capacities of students.

A second corollary which my analysis of critical thinking tried to take into account was the fact that an effective thinker in one area is not necessarily an effective thinker in all other areas. For example, while Einstein could communicate remarkably in physics, he was rather inept at poetry. I have suggested that this is because the knowledge and skills required for the one activity are quite different from the knowledge and skills required for the other. And while it is possible that one person can be quite accomplished at many different activities, common sense suggests such a person possesses several different kinds of knowledge and understanding: it is not one skill, generically referred to as "reasoning," which one then uniformly applies to all these tasks. It is possible that there may be some common elements in the various tasks requiring reasoning, but a little reflection suggests that the differences among the kinds of reasoning are far greater, and more obvious, than whatever they may have in common. After the fact, a logician might want to describe some inference by an historian as "inductive," as he might also describe some mathematician's or astronomer's inference as "inductive," but this logical nomenclature is merely a handy theoretical (or formal) description of the two inferences. It is not meant to suggest that the knowledge and skills required for making these inferences are in any way identical. Moreover, almost all of the empirical studies which have searched for transfer-of-training effects, particularly in the cognitive domain, have been notoriously unpromising to say the least. This result, I suggest, is what common sense would predict. My analysis of critical thinking tries to take these considerations into account. But the Informal Logic Movement, by contrast, continues to press for its small bag of tricks (e.g., the fallacies, etc.) to make one a critical thinker in any area no matter what the subject matter.

The final commonsense property of critical thinking that I tried to account for was that what we typically mean when we say that someone is a critical thinker is that they somehow think for themselves; they do not simply believe everything which they may hear or read. I have argued that such people have both the disposition (or propensity) and the relevant knowledge and skills to engage in an activity with reflective skepticism. That is, not only are they prone to question things, but they have the relevant knowledge and understanding to help them do so productively. And if one thinks long enough about what this might entail, particularly from a curriculum point of view, I suggest you will find that its major ingredients are close to what we have always thought of as a good liberal education. There are ways of improving this kind of education, and hence, critical thinkers, but there are no shortcuts to it. This is because the various "forms of thought" (to use Paul Hirst's phrase) have a logic, texture, and relevant background knowledge which are peculiar to themselves. And a course or two called "critical thinking" cannot begin to capture these relevant peculiarities.

In sum, I take these points to be a matter of common sense to any who take the time to think about it. As promised, they contain nothing mysterious nor esoteric. Yet each of them is incompatible with, and flies in the face of, the standard or most common approaches to critical thinking to be found in the literature (particularly the Informal Logic Movement). Each of these commonsense points is either denied, or somehow swept under the rug, by the informal-logic approach to critical thinking. If I were to put my basic disagreement with the Informal Logic Movement into one bold-relief sentence, it is this: in their attempt to develop critical thinking, they have the order of cause and effect reversed. They believe that if you train students in certain logical skills (e.g., the fallacies, etc.), the result will be a general improvement in each of the other disciplines or qualities of mind. Whereas I contend that if we improve the quality of understanding through the disciplines (which may have little to do with "logic" directly), you will then get a concomitant improvement in critical thinking capacity. When the difference between us is put this way, one might be tempted to ask, "Are these two approaches really all that incompatible?" Well, put this way, no, they are not *logically* incompatible. But from a pedagogic and practical point of view they are clearly at odds, because, to me, they have the tail wagging the dog. They make much the same error as teaching someone how to use a computer by teaching them only what all computer languages may have in common, and then leaving the rest to chance or personal interest. Whereas I would suggest teaching people how to program in the various computer languages, and leave whatever these languages may have in common to chance or personal interest. From an instructional point of view such a difference makes all the difference.

Critical thinking: "general ability" or "specific skills"?

I would now like to look at critical thinking from a slightly different perspective, a more psychological perspective. I want to consider the question of just what kind of thing it is that one has when one can think critically. Specifically, is it some kind of *general ability,* such as, say, verbal ability, or perhaps intelligence? Or is it rather more like a *specific skill* which can be directly taught, and which the person can then either do or not do depending on whether they have been taught that skill? This difference is sometimes described by psychologists as the difference between a "general aptitude" and a "specific skill."

It is important to raise this kind of question for two reasons. First, if we have a fairly clear idea of what kind of competence it is, then we should have some better ideas of how to teach and test for it, and we should have more realistic expectations of what courses designed to promote critical thinking might hope to accomplish. The second reason this kind of question is important is that several government reports and prestigious commissions have strongly recommended that schools start teaching people to be critical thinkers, yet neither they nor the programs which they have spawned are at all clear about what kind of thing critical thinking *is,* nor what these initiatives are supposed to accomplish. There is, therefore, no clear acid test for the success or failure of these expensive programs.

A review of the literature on critical thinking tests reveals a fairly clear body of opinion which treats critical thinking as a "general ability" that can be measured independently of context and subject matter. The *Watson-Glaser Critical Thinking Appraisal* is perhaps the best known, but I know of at least twenty-six other tests designed to measure critical thinking ability and which also treat critical thinking as a general ability. My purpose here is not so much to criticize these tests *per se,* but to draw out some of the implications of conceptualizing critical thinking as a generalized ability, as these tests seem to do.

If we take the Watson-Glaser test as a typical example, a perusal of the accompanying test manual clearly reveals that critical thinking is to be thought of as a "general ability" and not a specific skill. The discussion in the manual makes plain that the test is committed to three propositions:

1. that the ability to perform on the test items is content- and context-free; that is, no specific knowledge or information is required. The test items themselves provide all the required information.
2. as the manual explicitly states, that *critical thinking ability* is a *composite* of five sub-abilities:
    (i)   the ability to define a problem;
    (ii) the ability to select pertinent information for the solution of a problem;
    (iii) the ability to recognize stated and unstated assumptions;

(iv) the ability to formulate and select relevant and promising hypotheses;

(v) the ability to draw valid conclusions and judge the validity of inferences;

3. that the test is measuring a unique or *sui generis* human ability (albeit a composite one).

These propositions almost define what is usually meant by a general ability.

Now, if we consider critical thinking to be the kind of general ability that Watson and Glaser's test purports to measure, then we can begin to notice several things about it. First, we might notice that, given the description of the abilities involved and their context-free measurements, *critical thinking* turns out to be very similar to what we normally mean by general scholastic ability, or *intelligence*. That is, not only are critical thinking and intelligence both supposed to be general abilities, but in this case they look very much like *the same* general ability. From a conceptual point of view, it is difficult even to imagine a person being able to score well on one of these tests without also being able to score well on the other—particularly when one remembers that the items on both tests are designed to be relatively content- and context-free. And if critical thinking is the kind of content-free general ability that Watson and Glaser appear to think it is, at least two things follow: (1) it is not at all clear what the test is measuring apart from intelligence, and (2) we should be leery of programs purporting to teach it directly given the recalcitrance of IQ to improvement by direct teaching. The variance on IQ seems to remain substantial despite massive compensatory education programs. This is not to suggest that *bona fide* critical thinking can never be improved, but it is to suggest that there may be something *conceptually* limiting in considering it to be a "content-free general ability."

On the *empirical* side, things are even worse for Watson and Glaser's conception of critical thinking. They cite the high correlation coefficients with various intelligence tests as an index of the critical thinking tests' validity. In effect, they are saying: bright people tend to score well in the critical thinking appraisal. (Draw your own inference if you do poorly!) But Watson and Glaser are trying to have it both ways, it seems to me. They want to cite the tests' high correlations with general intelligence as a psychometric virtue, yet they want to claim that they are measuring something *else* (i.e., some *other* general ability). However, if they are measuring something quite distinct from intelligence, then we should be able to find cases of people with low IQ yet high critical thinking ability, and conversely we should find people with high IQ and low critical thinking ability. As I have pointed out elsewhere, however, even according to Watson and Glaser's own norming data, this doesn't happen. The situation with critical thinking tests and IQ is analogous to the situation between "creativity" and IQ, *viz.*, they correlate so highly with one another that they appear to be measuring one thing and not two distinct things. Watson and Glaser's conception of "critical thinking," like "creativity," would appear to have little discriminant validity. For these reasons, then, I suggest that critical thinking is not a content-free general ability, and, furthermore, we should be skeptical about educational programs and initiatives which assume that it is.

There is, however, a competing conception of critical thinking in the literature that conceives of it as a small set of specific skills which, once learned, can be applied in any area requiring critical thought. This view of critical thinking is predominant amongst those advocating informal-logic programs for critical thinking. In fact, some of these programs use the phrases *informal logic* and *critical thinking* more or less interchangeably, as though this is what "critical thinking" obviously *meant*. Perhaps I should reiterate that none of the views discussed here is particularly clear about precisely what kind of an ability critical thinking is. There is a considerable amount of slipping and sliding over this question. So one has to dig beneath the surface, as it were, in order to unearth what is meant by critical thinking ability.

In the case of the informal-logic approach, one can see certain similarities to and certain differences from the "general ability" approach. (Perhaps this is what renders the slipping and sliding so tempting at times.) The major *difference* embedded in the "specific skills" view (e.g., the informal-logic approach) is that critical thinking consists in a relatively small number of specific teachable skills which, once mastered, enable one to deploy these skills across any problems, arguments, or questions where critical thinking might be called for. On this view, those who have had the advantage of the specific training will be much more capable of critical thought than those who have not. The major *similarity* of this view with the "general ability" view is that these specific skills are likewise content- and context-free, and can therefore be deployed generally across different subjects and tasks.

Incidentally, informal-logic teachers frequently report large gains on the Watson-Glaser test following courses in informal logic. (I confess to similar findings myself in years past.) And this finding tends to reinforce the belief that critical thinking is developed by mastering their specific skills. They take such results as clear evidence for the necessity of their specific skills for critical thinking. However, there are at least two reasons why such results should not be taken too seriously. The first is that there is so much overlap between the Watson-Glaser test items and what is taught in these informal-logic courses that it amounts to direct training or "coaching." Thus, improved results are hardly surprising. Second, no evidence that I know of comes near to establishing that such direct skill-training can be transferred to examples or situations unlike those on the test. Thus, there is a curious kind of mutual propping-up exercise going on between the Watson-Glaser test and the specific skills which are allegedly required for critical thinking.

The difficulty that I have with the "specific skills" view of critical thinking is that these putative skills appear to be neither *necessary* nor *sufficient* for true critical thinking, and that there is a much more plausible view that is congruent with our commonsense intuitions about critical thinking. That certain specific skills are *not necessary* for critical thinking is evidenced by the fact that many people can and do display critical thinking who have never been directly taught, and perhaps have never heard of, the specific skills supposedly required of critical thinkers. As the Watson-Glaser norm data shows, people with conventional liberal arts educations tend to score highest on their test; and there is little reason to believe that these people have been directly trained in any of these specific skills (e.g., the informal fallacies, etc.). Second, if certain specific skills were necessary for critical thinking, then you would expect to find that only those people with the requisite training are able to do it. What we find, however, is that it appears to be normally distributed, just as IQ is.

To show that certain specific skills are also not sufficient for critical thinking would require an analysis of the specific skills alleged to compose it. Unfortunately, the list of specific skills is subject to change from program to program. However, all the specific skills that I have seen, and those mentioned on the Watson-Glaser test are typical, turn out not to be skills at all. For example, consider two of the putative "skills" included by Watson and Glaser in their definition of "critical thinking": (1) the ability to select pertinent information for the solution of a problem; (2) the ability to formulate and select relevant and promising hypotheses.

I submit that while the grammar of these phrases might suggest that *bona fide* abilities are being described, upon analysis, they do not describe any singular or specific abilities at all, but rather they describe large collections of different kinds of skills and abilities. They are rather like "the ability to win at games"; it doesn't matter what kind of game, any game from tiddly-winks to chess, and football to cricket: "the ability to win at games" means just what it says. But there is no specific ability or skill to win all kinds of games. Rather, there are literally hundreds of skills and kinds of skills involved. And so it is with Watson and Glaser's "ability to select pertinent information for the solution of a problem." Does this mean any and all problems? And aren't "problems" and their solutions at least as diverse as games? The moral to be drawn from this is that these phrases do not really denote true abilities at all, let alone specific ones. If they were describing specific abilities, then you should be able to train a person in that specific skill and it could then be deployed on all other problems (or games). Thus, such phrases as these often masquerade as describing specific abilities, but we should not be seduced by the grammar of such talk, because further analysis usually reveals that they are not *one* but *many* abilities or skills.

However, setting aside these conceptual difficulties for a moment, let us suppose that there are certain directly trainable skills which we believe to be important to critical thinking somehow (say, for example, the informal fallacies). There remain two important questions which we would have to answer about these skills. The first is, are they really as broadly deployable across all or most questions requiring critical thought as we might initially think? We should be aware that this question is not merely an empirical question about the transfer of training across multiple domains and contexts, but more importantly it is a question about the different kinds or reasoning which are ingredient in, and characterize, the different domains of knowledge. That is, scientific thinking or mathematical thinking would appear to be substantially different from moral thinking or literary thinking. Not only are the canons of validity different, but what might be fallacious reasoning in one context or domain, might be perfectly correct in another. This fact about the different forms of thought casts serious doubt about the interfield validity of any small set of specific trainable skills. However, even if we could find some common elements of reasoning that apply equally across fields or domains, we would still have to ask whether these common elements are sufficient to enable one to make the required critical judgments that various problems require.

My own view is that these common or specific skills account for such a small portion of the total reasoning required vis-à-vis the complex of cognitive demands posed by different problems, that they are far from sufficient for regarding a person as a critical thinker in all (or even most) domains. Just as knowing how to spell and to type would be nowhere near sufficient for writing philosophy essays or literary criticism, so these specific skills would be nowhere near sufficient for *bona fide* critical thinking across multiple domains. The vast array of problems, and types of understanding required, are simply too diverse to regard any set of specific skills sufficient for critical thinking in all or even most of them. And when one stops to consider that most problems or questions which require critical thought (e.g., public issues, etc.) are complexes, or combinations, of different types of knowledge and understanding, then the sufficiency of any set of specific skills appears even more remote and unlikely.

The second question which must be faced by any claim that certain specific skills are sufficient for critical thinking is this: what is the major ingredient of critical thinking? Is it having knowledge and understanding, or is it having certain specific skills? Here again, I am afraid, I must appeal to your common, everyday experience. When, for example, there is a discussion or argument about some public issue, be it the war in El Salvador, disarmament, Reaganomics, or what have you, who is usually

Plato

able to make the more useful contribution? Is it the person who possesses the relevant knowledge and information, or is it the person who has been trained in certain specific skills? If your experience has been anything like mine, it is the person who has the relevant knowledge. Incidentally, for those of you familiar with Michael Scriven's treatment of *extended arguments* (in his book *Reasoning*), where he is trying to teach the skills of "argument analysis," you might notice that these arguments are usually resolved by bringing into the argument some additional relevant information or knowledge not given in the original argument. We should notice this is not a matter of skill, but again, a matter of knowledge.

For these reasons, then, I submit that possessing certain specific skills is neither *necessary* nor *sufficient* for true critical thinking, and that it is unproductive to conceive of it this way.[1]

The "Trivial Pursuit" theory of knowledge

Since I have argued that critical thinking is not a content-free "general ability," nor is it a set of "specific skills," I suppose you think it time that I come out of the closet and declare what kind of cognitive entity I think critical thinking is. After all, if I'm opposed to monogamy and polygamy, I must be in favor of something. So what is it? I shall try to oblige this question in a moment. But my answer will be more clearly understood if I contrast it with an assumption which I think underlies both of the views discussed above. This assumption consists of a certain view about knowledge and facts which I shall call the "Trivial Pursuit" theory of knowledge. I call it this because both views tend to treat the substantive knowledge and information for critical thinking as though it typically consisted of facts which are relatively simple and discrete. Like the game Trivial Pursuit, knowledge is assumed to be the kind of thing which can be fitted into one-sentence questions, with one-sentence answers. Moreover, such knowledge is more or less unambiguous, noncontroversial, and conceptually simple. Television quiz shows exploit this same type of knowledge. The reason that the standard views of critical thinking unwittingly treat knowledge in this same way is that it is only by holding substantive knowledge constant, and unproblematic, that direct training in their skills or abilities takes on any plausibility. The operative strategy seems to be: first you get the relevant facts (and as in quiz shows, this step is assumed to be relatively straightforward), and *then* you use these various skills to derive clever solutions or arguments. Since knowledge is usually assumed to be common knowledge (e.g., "everyday knowledge"), as in quiz shows, all that one needs to be a critical thinker is to have facility with certain skills and abilities. This assumption about knowledge pervades the simplistic textbook examples designed to teach reasoning skills. All the relevant knowledge is given in the premises, and one is taught how to draw appropriate conclusions from it. The knowledge itself is always assumed to be complete and nonproblematic. In real life, however, this assumption about knowledge cannot be maintained. For actual problems, the required knowledge is seldom complete, almost always problematic, and susceptible to several interpretations.

Moreover, the criteria for what should count as relevant knowledge are themselves problematic. The relevant knowledge cannot be assumed to be complete or obvious. And a person's critical assessment of things, such as knowledge claims, etc., will necessarily be influenced by their experience, understanding, cognitive perspective, and values. The knowledge component of critical thinking will not stand still, as it were, but is constantly being added to, reinterpreted, and assessed from different perspectives. This complex processing of knowledge is always involved in real-life problems which require critical thought, and it is the *norm,* not the *exception.* The only instances where this complex processing of knowledge is not required is when the knowledge is assumed to be complete and unproblematic, as in the simple textbook examples, or in Trivial Pursuit. But such problems are themselves trivial, and hardly require critical thought. It is only by denigrating or ignoring the complexities of substantive knowledge and information that the specific-skills approach can be made to even sound initially plausible. They treat knowledge as a kind of simple "recall," or simply something essentially mindless.

The intimate connection between the *kinds of knowledge* and their corresponding *kinds of skills* helps to clarify my view of critical thinking. I would now like to state my view as succinctly as I can. First, it includes a *knowledge component,* that is, knowledge-based skills whose general range of applicability is limited by the form of thought or kind of knowledge being called upon. The second component, which we might regard as the specifically *critical component,* consists of the ability to reflect upon, to question effectively, and to suspend judgment or belief about the required knowledge composing the problem at hand. This critical component, it should be noted, is parasitic upon the knowledge component since the epistemic status (i.e., its certainty and its vulnerability) of the different kinds of knowledge varies considerably. That is, there are some data, say, that enjoy a much higher degree of certainty and reliability than others. All so-called data is not on an equal footing. The critical thinker, therefore, knows what and when it might be reasonable to question something. But this requires comprehensive understanding of the kind of information that it is, and perhaps how it is gathered or generated. Critical thinking ability, therefore, varies directly with the amount of knowledge required by the problem. Enough, then, about the cognitive ingredients of critical thinking.

The purpose of critical thinking

Since it is theoretically possible to train people for critical thinking in very narrow domains and practical tasks, just as it is for very broad domains and theoretical tasks, we therefore have to ask ourselves *what kind* of critical thinking we are interested in developing. For *whom* and for *what*? Certain kinds of knowledge and information will lay the groundwork for critical thinking about some kinds of problems but not others. And since school time and human capacities are limited, choices have to be made. Such choices will reflect society's values and the very purpose of public schooling. Here enters the normative side of education. It is not a value-neutral enterprise.

In our society, at least since the time of Thomas Jefferson, the chief purpose of schools has been to produce an informed citizenry, capable of making intelligent decisions about the problems which might face it. Ostensibly, we would like students to become critical thinkers for every such problem, and perhaps more personal ones as well. But when one reflects upon both the diversity and complexity of such problems, in the present as well as the future, the goal is nothing short of staggering. The briefest list would include such diverse problems as the morality of abortion, pornography, and minority rights, the multidimensions of pollution, nuclear disarmament, the feasibility and equality of various taxation schemes, television hype and propaganda, etc., etc., etc. When one considers how complex and knowledge-dependent rational solutions really are for any one of these problems, the odds against a sufficiently informed citizenry are almost demoralizing. Indeed, the odds finally led Walter Lippmann to conclude (in his book *Public Opinion*), after forty-five years of covering public issues from Washington, that the democratic citizenry is no longer up to the task of adequately responding to the increased complexity of the problems that face it. Gone are the days of "the town meeting," he argued. Increasing complexity of contemporary problems makes appeal to "the experts" and their technocracy inevitable. Similar observations led Carl L. Becker to say, "Round every next corner democracy works less well than it did." This circumstance might also explain why modern mass communication largely consists of image making and slogans rather than clear explanations of the issues: the real issues, and real explanations, are too complex for mass consumption. So, as in advertising, the catchy phrase or image increasingly forms our views on reality.

All of this, believe it or not, is not intended as a "doom or gloom" prophecy for democracy. The practical alternatives to an informed citizenry remain as abhorrent to us now as they did to Thomas Jefferson. The point is simply to dramatize the enormity of the task that one sets for oneself when one says, "Let's make critical thinkers out of our students." To perceive the task from this perspective helps to explain why quick-fix solutions for the critical thinking problem are so tempting to some people: one or two courses in the right critical thinking skills, and most of these problems can be handled—at least so the rhetoric goes. However, the main point of looking at critical thinking from this broader perspective is that it underscores the real limitations which any critical thinking program is bound to have. Since we could not possibly provide the requisite knowledge for every kind of problem, we are forced to ask the most fundamental of all curriculum questions: what kind of knowledge is most worthwhile for our students? Given the kinds of problems which are imbedded in the Jeffersonian ideal of an informed citizenry, we can see that any answer to this question must involve some very broad domains of understanding.

Another way of putting this basic curriculum question is, what kinds of knowledge and understanding are likely to have the most universal value? When the question is put this way, notice, it is not a question about transfer-of-training effects, which is a psychological question, but a question about what kinds of knowledge we consider to possess the most value. Will it be, for example, how to repair one's automobile, or the study of history? Will it be public speaking or literature? These are the sorts of questions that must be faced for education in general and *a fortiori* for critical thinking in particular.

It seems to me, therefore, that when all of these points are taken into consideration, there is no other plausible candidate for our curriculum besides a broad liberal education. No other curriculum can provide quite the same breadth of understanding into the human condition and the problems which perennially face it. The disciplines which make up a liberal education (e.g., those in the arts, the sciences, and humanities) are not separate from, nor alien to, the everyday problems requiring critical thought, but rather they are the fundamental constituents of such problems. To attempt to think rationally at all is to employ the various forms of rational discourse which are the disciplines. This, indeed, is the core of Paul Hirst's defense of a liberal education. However, there has come to be a strong and widely held belief that standard disciplinary knowledge is somehow technical, esoteric, abstract, or primarily of academic interest. This view fails to recognize that the disciplines had their origins in the human condition and are substantively about the human condition. Their *raison d'être* is to provide insight and under-standing into the problems faced by humanity. If the disciplines are believed to consist in merely esoteric or academic knowledge, then this says more about the poor way this knowledge is perhaps often taught, but this should not confuse us about the basic purpose and power of the disciplines. Despite rhetoric to the contrary, the disciplines do not exist for their own sake. Rather, they enable rational discourse about the problems which confront us. It is the job of educators to convey this power and purpose of the disciplines because they are the basic ingredients of rationality itself.

Having reasserted the case for the liberal arts as the most efficacious vehicle for critical thinking, two further clarifications must be emphatically stressed. First, I am not claiming that typical, everyday problems of the sort we are interested in will always, or indeed *ever,* fall neatly into one domain or the other. The typical problem is many-faceted and multidimensional, therefore several types of knowledge and understanding will be needed for most problems. I am simply claiming that because the disciplines provide knowledge and understanding which goes "beyond the present and the particular" (to use Charles Bailey's felicitous phrase), they provide the best set of knowledge and skills for coping with problems affecting society.

The second point which must be stressed about liberal education is that it does not consist in merely taking in or absorbing a lot of different types of information; its major characteristics is that it enables one to understand and appreciate both the strengths and weaknesses, and the power and limitations, of the various forms of thought which make up our thinking. That is, the liberally educated student should understand the epistemic status of different types of knowledge claims within the different forms of knowledge. Liberal education is not, of course, the passive acquisition of different types of information, as it is being able to enter the various forms of rational discourse as an autonomous thinker. The liberally educated person must understand the different *processes* of reasoning every bit as much as the *products* of the reasoning. Moreover, such a person is not someone who merely possesses arcane knowledge in a half a dozen specialty areas, but rather one who possesses a broad cognitive perspective (to borrow a phrase from R. S. Peters) which enables him to see significance in the most mundane events.

The proponents of various courses in critical thinking will often say, at this point, that they have never denied the value of liberal education, and that they have no desire to displace it. Rather, they typically make either or both of two claims to justify their courses. One claim is that liberal arts courses seldom if ever contain so-called everyday problems and everyday reasoning within their syllabi; thus critical thinking courses are designed to compensate this deficiency. The other claim often made is that these courses are intended to specifically teach people how to think critically, as such, within and about the disciplines. Both of these claims for critical thinking courses justify their purpose as a kind of topping-up exercise designed to offset or rectify the perceived deficiencies of the liberal arts curriculum.

If we disregard those deficiencies which are due to poor or inadequate teaching, since these are present in any kind of program, it seems to me that both these claims for critical thinking courses misrepresent or misunderstand the nature of liberal education and what it is intended to do. The first claim, that liberal education fails to teach reasoning about "everyday problems,"simply fails to appreciate that this is precisely what the disciplines are about—the disciplines simply study these problems one dimension at a time. And the second claim for critical thinking courses, that it teaches how to be critical within the disciplines themselves, fails to recognize that the standards and criteria for rational thinking are uniquely determined by the disciplines themselves, and not by some external criterion.

The strongest case that I have heard made for critical thinking courses is that they can serve a kind of remedial role for those whose education has been otherwise so inadequate that they are seriously deficient in any kind of autonomous thinking. To give credit where it is due, perhaps such courses can help to remedy this. But we should recognize that this is a rear-guard action and not the vanguard of a new and promising curriculum for all. The glitter of such programs is for those with little light to begin with. Even in these cases I would suggest the more direct remedy of improving the quality of the normal curriculum, where teachers feel more at home, rather than laying on yet another specific course in an already crowded curriculum.

How to improve critical thinking

It may not be obvious, I'm afraid, but there is a point to my leading you through these disagreements about the nature of critical thinking. The point is a very practical one—namely, we should now have a better idea of what is involved in teaching for critical thinking. If there is any truth to my view that critical thinking skills are primarily dependent upon, even peculiar to, the various forms of rational discourse (e.g., morality, art, science, history, etc.), then at least two conclusions follow: (1) that general courses in critical thinking are either over-zealous or simple-minded since, unlike Trivial Pursuit, the relevant knowledge is not all cut from the same conceptual cloth; and (2) that the so-called thinking skills are an inherent part of the warp and woof of the various disciplines, and must, therefore, be taught as part of them.

Happily, most teachers are already fairly knowledgeable in their parent disciplines, at least in secondary schools and beyond, so there really is no need for an entirely new specialty, or alien expertise, in order to improve critical thinking skills in their classes. It requires more of a shift in emphasis, or redesigning their material and tests to reflect this emphasis on independent thinking. I am not claiming that teachers are now capable of doing this effectively on their own, but I do suggest that with a little guidance and a few suggestions, teachers are already more than half-way there by virtue of their understanding of their discipline.

The really useful and concrete suggestions for teachers would, of course, have to be discipline-specific (e.g., how to improve historical thinking skills). Here, you will appreciate, I have neither the space nor the competence to provide suggestions for each of the disciplines. But I can at least indicate two potentially rich sources of suggestions for each of the disciplines. Both of these sources might provide the necessary skills and understanding required for critical thinking. The University of Chicago's Joseph Schwab once described this understanding as follows:

> Let [a body of knowledge] be taught in such a way that the student learns what substantive structures gave rise to the chosen body of knowledge, what the strengths and limitations of these structures are, and what some of the alternatives are which give rise to alternative bodies of knowledge.[2]

One source which could help a teacher provide this kind of understanding to students can be found in the "philosophy of" their specific discipline. Many teachers are not even aware that such a philosophical literature exists for their own discipline. But much of this literature consists in explaining and laying bare, as it were, the epistemic foundations and logical peculiarities of the various disciplines. If teachers possessed this fresh and somewhat different perspective on their discipline, they could better see what kinds of questions and material would give rise to this kind of understanding. As a starting place and general guide to this literature, I would first recommend reading a very clear and important paper by Israel Scheffler entitled "Philosophies-of and the Curriculum" (in *Educational Judgments,* edited by James F. Doyle, London, [RKP, 1973]). This paper provides an exceptionally clear rationale for using this literature, and describes what teachers can hope to get from it for teaching the structure and logic of their discipline.

In addition to the "philosophy-of" literature, there are many discipline-specific monographs by educators which are extremely perceptive about the logical and conceptual peculiarities of their field. And many of these monographs contain useful pedagogic strategies for making these peculiarities manifest to students. The names, indeed disciplines, are too numerous to list here, but I have in mind the kind of work that, say, Gerald Holton has done in physics education, and Schwab in biology, Northrop Frye in literature, and Elliot Eisner in art education. Much of this kind of literature can take teachers a long way toward teaching critical thinking in their respective fields.

The medievals used to say that there is nothing really new under the sun. And I realize that I have said nothing that is really new. But sometimes old ideas remain good ideas and need another day on top— particularly when there are so many bad ideas seeking to displace them.

CHAPTER 3

Teaching critical thinking through the disciplines

As my title suggests, I intend to defend the view that the standard (or familiar) disciplines are the most direct route, if not the *only* efficacious route, to teaching critical thinking. A consequence of this view is that most of the so-called thinking skills programs, which are so pervasive today, are importantly misguided. My express purpose here, however, is *not* to criticize thinking skills programs, but rather to constructively show the ways in which disciplinary knowledge already contains the major portion of what most people understand by "critical thinking." In short, I argue that if the disciplines are properly taught, we will get the kind of intelligent thought from students that we normally associate with the phrase *critical thinking*. Thus, training and drills in the so-called thinking skills are effectively redundant. I argue that reasoning skill is not something different from, or over and above, disciplinary thinking (as is implied by the "thinking skills" movement), but is in fact part and parcel of disciplinary thinking.

Thus, I too call for reform, or improvement, in education. We can indeed do much better than at present. But I do not support the revolution that is implicit in the recent thinking skills movement, because to construe the problem of critical thinking as a matter of improved "skills and drills" is to misunderstand what is involved in rational thinking in general, and critical thinking in particular.

Although I will not discuss the details of any particular thinking skills program, I will refer to what I have generally referred to as the thinking skills movement. I mean by this label such programs as, Feurstein's *Instructional Enrichment Program,* De Bono's *Cort Thinking Lessons,* the *Productive Thinking Program, Odyssey,* typical informal logic courses, and most of the thinking skills programs surveyed in the large, two-volume study conducted for the National Institute of Education edited by J. Segal, S. Chipman, and R. Glaser entitled *Thinking and Learning Skills* (Hillsdale, New Jersey, 1985). What all of these programs and approaches have in common is a commitment to the view that the *process* of reasoning should take precedence over the *content* of what is being reasoned about. It is not that specific content is irrelevant in the thinking skills view, but rather that teachers should concentrate their attention on the teaching of the reasoning *process* as such. These programs are thus how-to-do-it approaches; and this orientation helps to explain their emphasis on skills and drills of one kind or another.

Before I discuss an alternative disciplines approach to all of this, it may be useful to keep in mind several points of agreement between my view and the thinking skills approach. To begin with, we agree on ultimate goals and purposes. We all want to produce autonomous thinkers who are not taken in by faulty argument, weak evidence, or "trendy" opinions, and can face life's problems as people capable of making their own rational decisions about whatever should confront them. These problems and decisions include personal and societal problems, as well as those we might normally think of as academic or cognitive problems. In short, we all want to enable students to become the maximally rational human beings that they are capable of being. Moreover, we agree that this capability can and should be taught to students (whenever possible), since they are not born with the requisite knowledge and skill for attaining this goal. Also, on a more practical instructional level, we agree that the attitude of the teacher, and the learning atmosphere in the class, is likely to have real and important effects on the success of nurturing such autonomous thinking. And finally, we agree that ignorance, indoctrination, and unreflective conformity are the enemy.

This much agreement is all to the good, and should not be minimized: we agree on our destination, but disagree on the best route for getting there. Similarly, however, we should not minimize the serious consequences of choosing an alternative route, because it might not lead to our destination, despite the best intentions.

The alternative route to our destination which I propose begins early on. I wish to redirect attention away from generic *processes of reasoning,* be these logical skills or general strategies, and to have you consider the proposition that the *content* of various subjects and/or problems determines (i.e., creates) the appropriate *process* of reasoning, and not vice versa. Thus, I would have teachers and researchers consider early on how various kinds of knowledge and understanding of things appropriately shape the way people properly think about those things (this, rather than looking for generic "skills" which are alleged to be subject-neutral).

The theoretical underpinning for looking at reasoning from this perspective is to be found in Wittgenstein's insight about the very intimate connection between *thought* and *language.* For Wittgenstein, anything which you or I would recognize as significant thought is fundamentally linguistic in character. (Or more precisely, if the *thought* is not in *words,* as such, it will be in some kind of public symbol system—which is most often language.) Thus, to improve people's capacity for thought, you must improve their capacity to use language. The capacity for sophisticated, complex, or subtle thought proportionately requires the sophisticated, complex, or subtle use of a symbol system—which is usually language. And since language can be used for many and diverse purposes, there are many and diverse "rules" of predication (or "language-games") which govern what can and cannot be coherently thought or said. It is not enough, from this point of view, to know that different objects can take different predicates—this is trivially true. We must come to understand what kinds of things in the world can take what kinds of predicates, and what kinds of combinations (or attributions) are and are not coherent ideas. Just as there are different kinds of "language-games," which stem from what Wittgenstein called different "forms of life" (e.g., mathematics, morality, religion, art, etc.), so there are different rules of predication, or "reasoning," if you will, which govern the different kinds of thought.[1]

To put this very, very crudely, different subjects employ different language-games, and different language-games have their own peculiar (or unique) rules of predication. How sentences can and cannot be put together constitutes the first level logic of that particular language-game. A bit more formally, the actual rules for what is a "well-formed formula" (i.e., an intelligible statement) is determined at the *semantic* level of discourse. Thus, there are almost as many distinguishable logics, or kinds of reasoning, as there are distinguishable kinds of subjects. And there is no way to learn these different logics apart from learning the language (or meanings) of those subjects. This is why I argue that real, honest-to-goodness everyday reasoning is intimately and permanently connected to the different subjects—more specifically to the language of those subjects. Neil Postman also expresses this view when he points out:

> As one learns the language of a subject, one is also learning what that subject is. It cannot be said often enough that what we call a subject consists mostly, if not entirely, of its language. If you eliminate all the words of a subject, you have eliminated the subject. Biology is not plants and animals. It is language about plants and animals. History is not events. It is language describing and interpreting events. Astronomy is not planets and stars. It is a way of talking about planets and stars.

He continues:

> If one learns how to speak history or mathematics or literary criticism, one becomes, by definition, a different person. The point to be stressed is that a subject is a situation in which and through which people conduct themselves, largely in language. You cannot learn a new form of conduct without changing yourself. (*Teaching as a Conserving Activity,* pp. 165 – 67) [Delacorte, 1979]

I am arguing that this change which comes about is that a person begins to learn how to think and to reason through language. And this becomes progressively more sophisticated, or complex, as one learns more about a subject. In principle, at least, this is what the disciplines attempt to do, or are capable of doing. This is, in effect, an argument for liberal education through the disciplines: it *liberates* one by teaching him or her how to think.

Perhaps I should add here two qualifications, or cautionary notes, about the Wittgensteinian view about the connection between thought and language. First, what Wittgenstein refers to as a "language-game," and the rules governing these games, have a very similar function for thinking as Kant's "categories of the understanding." However, unlike Kant's categories, language-games are not fixed and immutable. Rather, Wittgenstein's categories are themselves determined by language, which are continually evolving to accommodate new demands brought on by changes in the different "forms of life." Thus, categories of understanding are not static (for Wittgenstein); but so long as they are in place at any given time, they constitute coherent thought.

The second feature to be noted about this view of language and thought is that while different language-games have their own peculiar rules of predication which are not determined by classical logic, these rules will, by and large, obey classical logic. That is, classical logic can be viewed as a system of meta-statements which can be asserted of language-games, but language-games are not themselves made up of these meta-statements. There is, as it were, a primary level of thinking which is governed by the semantic rules of language-games. This comprises the bulk of normal thinking behavior. Then there is also classical logic, which is *about* that thinking. From the point of view of actual use, however, classical logic, and skill at employing its rules, cannot yield the flesh and blood of everyday rational thought. It cannot do so for the same reasons that the *syntax* of a system cannot yield semantic *meaning*.

Now it might seem that we have moved some distance from our initial discussion about the "thinking skills movement" versus the "disciplinary" approach. But really we have not. The distinction between language-games and the rules of classical logic is simply a more abstract way of describing the parallel differences between a *content,* or disciplinary, approach to thinking from the numerous thinking skills programs. I am arguing that just as different "rules of predication" constitute different language-games, so different modes of reasoning constitute what we call "subject areas." Each is a different "category of understanding" (in a Wittgensteinian sense), and each has its own "rules," as it were, of reasoning. This is what renders a general thinking skills approach *implausible* from a theoretical point of view, and *ineffective* from a practical point of view—at least I so submit.

Before I develop the disciplinary (or language-game) approach a bit further, it is helpful to think about some of the factors which might have contributed to the popularity of the thinking skills movement, and some of the things which make it seem plausible to many. You will, of course, have to allow room for what I think is reasonable speculation here, because I cannot know precisely what factors have appealed to whom. But one very clear advantage that the thinking skills movement would "appear" to offer is relief from the very scary prospect of having to teach every fact about every plausible subject which might confront a student. *That* endeavor would indeed be impossible. Thus, if there *were* a set of general teachable skills, which could apply across the board, then we could simply arm students with these skills and turn them loose to face the complicated world. And this, indeed, is what the thinking skills movement promises.

However, there seems to be more wish-fulfillment at work here than there is reason to believe in its viability. It reminds me in several ways of President Reagan's fascination with his Star Wars scheme: it seems like a nice technological solution to what is in fact a very thorny political problem. Moreover, it seems to satisfy two quintessential American traits: (1) the love affair with technology (or gadgets), and (2) the feeling that every problem, no matter how complex, is fixable. This can-do spirit often prompts the familiar saw "If we can land a man on the moon, we can lick the drug problem" or "lick the crime problem," etc. In fact, however, it is not clear that all problems do have acceptable solutions, let alone technological ones. For example, if you believe that reason can construct a technological defense system, then you must have similar faith that reason is capable of cracking it—what's good for the goose is good for the gander. What is so powerful about reason is that it can very often tell you what *won't* work, even if it doesn't show you what will.

An additional explanation for the current enthusiasm for thinking skills programs derives from the widely held belief that *reasoning* is a learnable skill in the same way as, say, reading and writing. Indeed, numerous articles, and much talk, explicitly refer to reasoning as the "fourth R," along with reading, 'riting and 'rithmetic. All are perceived as general teachable skills—even though *reasoning* may be acknowledged to be slightly more complex than the other three R's. I think, however, that this widely held belief is as wrong about reading and writing as it is about reasoning. The general mistake stems from a seductive linguistic confusion, namely, that because we have a single word like *reading* or *writing,* and this word points out or refers to a single common property which is common to all cases of "reading" or "writing," the inference is made that this common property describes a single generic skill. However, all cases of "mending" have a common property also, namely, to fix whatever needs it, but to mend a fence, an auto engine, or a sock require very different skills. Not all generic skill words denote singular skills, and it is simply a mistake to think that they do.

Prompted by concern for declining reading scores, many researchers have been pointing out that even reading and writing are not general, transferable skills because they are crucially dependent on background knowledge—which varies from task to task. For example, E. D. Hirsch, the distinguished literary critic at the University of Virginia, recently described some of his own empirical studies with college students. He concluded:

> What these experiments demonstrate is that the idea that reading is a general, transferable skill unrelated to subject matter is essentially wrong, containing only the following grain of truth. Reading is a general skill only with regard to its rather elementary aspects, those involving phonics, parsing strategies, guessing strategies, eye habits, and so on. While these elementary skills are important, normally endowed students, once they acquire the rudiments, need not be continually drilled in them. Such skills are always being used, and every reading task will automatically exercise, improve, and automate them. With that single elementary exception, then, the usual picture of reading as a general skill is wrong. Reading skill varies from task to task, because reading skill depends on specific background knowledge. (*American Educator,* Summer 1985, p. 10)

This same conclusion about reading was reached by Neil Postman in *Teaching as a Conserving Activity:*

> To put it simply, the question "How well does one read?" is a bad question, because it is essentially unanswerable. A more proper question is "How well does one read poetry, or history, or religion?" No one I have ever known is so brilliant as to have learned the languages of all fields of knowledge equally well. Most of us do not learn some of them at all. No one is a "good reader," period. There are those, for example, who read the physical sciences well, but not poetry. Each discipline requires of the reader a particular set of abilities, store of knowledge, and frame of mind, so that there must always be great variability in our capacities to read, write, or speak in different subjects. (p. 164)

All of this suggests that there is serious reason to question the extent to which even reading and writing are general skills, let alone reasoning. What phonics, eye habits, and parsing strategies are to reading, classical logic is to reasoning; both are, indeed, general, but they won't get you through the practical task at hand.

From a more mundane point of view, there has been a tendency to think of reading, writing, and reasoning skill to be like typing, where you do, in fact, have a skill which can be ubiquitously used upon any subject matter. Once you can type, you can type anything and everything. But the crucial difference between typing and the four R's is that in typing you do not have to *understand* what is being typed. Once specific background knowledge is required as part of a skill, however, the *generality* of that skill is seriously restricted.

But let me return to my thesis that the disciplines embody the most efficacious route to critical thinking. Thus far, all I have done is to sketch the ways in which *thought* or thinking and *meaning* are connected to *language*. And I have suggested that language development is tantamount to the development of thought. Now, I argue that the net effect of *disciplinary knowledge* is to increase a student's capacity to think and to talk in the language of those disciplines. In effect, the disciplines enable one to think, and to engage in intelligent conversation, about problems which might fall under disciplinary domains. If we further conceive of the disciplines as more or less structured embodiments of the simple "forms of life" which give rise to them (*à la* Wittgenstein), one will see that much of what we regard as "common knowledge" and "everyday problems" are included within the disciplines. This is not to say that the disciplines have resolved, or provided answers to, the common or everyday problems; but it is to say that this is what they have been *about,* this was their origin, and this is what they have attempted to provide progressively more sophisticated insight into. It is not the case that we have academic or disciplinary knowledge on the one side, and *real* or everyday problems on the other. This is a false dichotomy. It is best to view common or everyday problems as the seeds which have spawned the disciplines. In a very real sense, the perennial problems which we now regard as common or everyday problems continue to be embodied within the disciplines. School knowledge is, after all, about the real world.

Again, this is not to suggest that disciplinary knowledge can solve all the problems requiring thought. To a large extent, problems and questions that we have will remain problems and questions, despite disciplinary knowledge. But I do want to make two important claims on behalf of the disciplines (and it is not at all clear that the thinking skills approach could make similar claims). First, the disciplines have, over the millennia, provided many important answers to important problems which used to perplex mankind. Indeed, many of these now constitute our cultural heritage; and this is, by and large, what the schools have been trying to pass on to students. Without this kind of education, each generation would be forced to reinvent the wheel—a highly dubious project. And the great bulk of this education comes via what we now think of as straightforward *content*. Second, through the use of their general concepts, and rich language, the disciplines provide a very powerful set of analytic lenses through which students can come to understand problems, and to grapple with them in rational ways. Indeed, what it means to be rational is to make decisions on the basis of the available evidence. And since people are not born knowing what evidence might be relevant for what, they must be taught. This is precisely what the disciplines attempt to do. In short, when the disciplines are effectively taught, they provide the most fundamental (and inescapable) cognitive requirements for being rational.

In recent years, educators have become enamored of the notion of "critical thinking," and all that it might imply. In fact, the critical thinking movement can be seen as the progenitor of the recent thinking skills movement. However, I think that if teachers and administrators would think carefully about what they may wish to achieve, they would see that *normal* rational thinking is more than adequate to meet their needs. Potentially, at least, the disciplines are already suited for the required job. There is no inherent reason for having to change their original strategy. Why, then, we might ask, did the schools feel the need to change their tack and begin introducing these new "skills" programs? I will answer this question momentarily, but my answer will be better understood in the light of a basic distinction between what I will call "normal correct thinking" (or standard *disciplinary* thinking) and critical thinking as such.

Many cognitive tasks, both in life and in school, have well-trodden paths to, or procedures for, their solution. For example, if you want to know the cheapest way to get from one city to another, you might look at a bus schedule, and learn to work your way through its columns of times and numbers—a relatively straightforward procedure. Or if you have a mathematical problem with three unknowns, you might be able to solve it by setting up three equations and then substituting values, one for another. In short, for very many problems which we confront, rational procedures often exist for their resolution. Some of these problems, of course, are more complex than others, and some require considerable background knowledge even to begin addressing them. Our culture, or more specifically the *disciplines,* have developed entire networks of concepts, methods, and procedures for dealing with an enormous spectrum of life's familiar (and unfamiliar) problems. They have developed tools, as it were, or kinds of tools, for dealing with many different kinds of problems. And even though these procedures may not ultimately be up to the task of solving any given problem, they still constitute the most rational procedure to trying, as a first approximation, to solve a problem. In effect, you should try all the tools in your kit before designing a new one for the particular job at hand. Traditionally, the public schools have been engaged in the business of trying to provide students with the knowledge and understanding contained in these disciplinary networks, concepts, and procedures. And I believe this to be a sensible goal, even if the level of understanding should not reach much beyond a beginner's level. At least students are beginners at the most worthwhile tools known to us as a culture. However, all of this knowledge is what I am here calling "normal" thinking or "correct" thinking or "familiar" thinking insofar as its patterns and procedures are more or less well entrenched in the culture. Mind you, to teach these things successfully is no mean achievement! Indeed, this educational outcome is what is normally meant by "rational thinking" *simpliciter*. This fact has led some commentators—specifically, Sophie Haroutunian (*Proceedings of the Philosophy of Education Society* 1985: 21–27)—to argue that this is really the kind of thinking that most educators are probably concerned about; and that the distinction between this kind of thinking and "critical thinking" is therefore a red herring—a difference not worth worrying about. Let me say that I am sympathetic to this view. If the schools could succeed in developing rational thinking, or normal disciplinary thinking, there would be far less talk and worry about "critical thinking" *per se*. Rational thinking would give us *almost all* of what we normally expect from our schools.

But for all this, critical thinking is not an empty concept. It does seem to refer to something which we also regard as worthwhile in people, and our language properly marks this out. I think that the phrase "critical thinking" refers to a certain *combination* of what we might think of as a willingness, or disposition (call it an "attitude," if you like), together with the appropriate knowledge and skills, to engage in an activity or problem with *reflective skepticism*. Critical thinking consists of the kind of healthy skepticism that we might normally associate with the discipline of philosophy. It is not pernicious skepticism, but rather the kind that we engage in when we have reason to suspect that the normal procedures, or beliefs, leave something to be desired. There might, indeed, be something in the normal procedures or beliefs which is creating the problem, rather than helping us solve it. Thus, critical thinking does not come into play on every occasion where rational thought is required, but only on those comparatively rare occasions where we suspect something is amiss. On such occasions it is right and proper to start questioning some of our fundamental assumptions, or beliefs, and to try alternatives: it is this kind of thinking which is properly described as "critical thinking"—and this is valuable indeed. But two characteristics of this kind of thinking must be borne in mind: (1) it is the exception, rather than the rule—normal rational procedures are often adequate for the task; and (2) it presupposes considerable knowledge of the subject area in question.

Thus, the distinction between "normal" rational thinking and "critical thinking" prompts the question of whether or not there has been undue worry about critical thinking as such. Perhaps Sophie Haroutunian is right. But even if one clings to the idea that critical thinking should somehow be woven into the fabric of our school system, because there is, after all, *something* to be said for the idea, there remain two important questions that do not have obvious answers: when should it be introduced, and how?

These two questions are closely connected, because if you conceive of critical thinking (as I do) as subject-specific, then *when* you introduce such a program is determined in large measure by *what* you are introducing. Since critical thinking is, in my view, parasitic upon the disciplines, it follows that you should not introduce it until students know something about the disciplines. Anything worthy of the name "critical thinking" cannot exist in a subject-matter vacuum. There must first be some substantive content for students to be critical about. Even if we could, in some sense, have young children produce behavior which resembles "critical thinking," surely there must be more pressing problems on our educational agendas at this early stage of their education. As the presidential report *A Nation At Risk* dramatically points out, the most fundamental deficiencies in American education are adequate literacy on the one hand, and basic information about what makes this culture on the other. Neither my view nor the president's report is a call to stifle independent and creative thought—far from it—but it is a call to get straight about what needs to be done *first*. You cannot have creative thought until there is some understanding of what one is being creative about. (You might get *original* thoughts, but that is not sufficient to make them *creative*.) It is simply bad pedagogy to teach exceptions before one understands the rule. Thus, it is unnecessary, and educationally premature, to teach critical thinking to young children. You don't race a pony until its legs are strong enough to take it. I would not, in fact, teach critical thinking before grade ten, or until such time as the disciplines have taken on noticeable shape as such. Then students have something worth sinking their teeth into, and in a way which would have meaningful point. Prior to that, it is love's labor being largely wasted, if not lost.[2]

There is a commonly heard objection to this view about waiting until high school, which runs something like the following: once children find out that school is a place where you simply absorb what the teacher says, they become more or less passive receptors of information who are *unable* to think critically because they have never been taught to do so. Thus, when you try to switch gears in high school, students will not be up to the task because they have had no practice, and will be adrift in this new mode of teaching. In other words, to wait until later, the argument runs, is too late.

This argument, plausible as it might appear to some, contains several unsubstantiated assumptions. The first is that most adults, including the authors of various thinking skills programs, have not, in fact, been permanently harmed by their early receptive learning. We made the shift in due course, and are none the worse for it. One often hears the assertion, however, that "I became an autonomous thinker *despite* the system, not because of it." But I am not at all sure about this, and I don't see how anyone else could be either. This assertion about one's educational past reminds me of a line in *Julius Caesar:* "one forgets the base degrees by which he did ascend." I think, to the contrary, that it is not only necessary to absorb passively information in the first stage in one's education, but it is also desired and enjoyed by children. Receptive learning of facts, and memorization, have perhaps taken an unjustifiable rap in education. As E. D. Hirsch has argued:

> In early grades, children are fascinated by straightforward information. Our official modern distaste for old-fashioned memorization and rote learning seems more pious than realistic. Young children are eager to master the materials essential for adult life, and if they believe in the materials they will proudly soak them up like sponges and never forget them . . . Young children have an urge to become acculturated into the adult world by learning the facts of the tribe long before they can make sense out of them. (*American Educator*, Summer 1985, p. 13)

To this day, one of my most memorable learning experiences came from fourth-grade geography, where we learned about the great explorers such as Marco Polo, Magellan, Cortez, and Drake. The tests on this material required straightforward memory work, but this did not detract from my interest and excitement in the subject matter. Indeed, most classes in those grades proceeded in the same didactic fashion. It is not at all clear to me that this was particularly harmful, nor that there is a better way to teach at this stage.

That young students might appear passive as a consequence of receptive learning is something to be taken in stride rather than worried about. To passively absorb information is the natural and appropriate way to learn that kind of material. There will be time for analysis and criticism in later grades, but first students must learn the basic information about their culture so that they will have something to be critical about. Possessing basic knowledge and information is a prerequisite for critical thinking, not a deterrent to it.

The contemporary distaste for memorization and receptive learning can, I think, be seen as an overreaction to fears of indoctrination. While this fear is understandable, it too is a red herring. No one advocates indoctrination; and there are important differences between indoctrination and receptive learning. To begin with, we are not talking about teaching doctrines as such, but rather the simplest facts about our world. Should some of these facts be regarded as importantly controversial, then, arguably, they could be pushed back to some later age when students are better prepared to cope with them. But more importantly, there are both conceptual and empirical differences between "indoctrination" and "receptive learning." The purpose and/or effect of *indoctrination* is that people come to hold a belief so firmly that they cannot change their mind about it even when confronted with counterevidence. However, the purpose and/or effect of *receptive learning* is to teach people what evidence is, so that they can learn to use evidence in the formation of their beliefs. While it is at least logically possible that a student could come to hold a belief unshakably even though it was not the teacher's intent, the only way to prevent that possibility would be to stop teaching altogether. Surely this would be a draconian solution; and I know of no one seriously advocating this. Moreover, the overwhelming facts are that most people do not become indoctrinated as a result of receptive learning. For every student who may have become permanently indoctrinated as a result of early receptive learning, I could show you thousands who have not. A person cannot even start on the path to a rational life without being given information, because information is a logically necessary ingredient of rationality.

Even setting the indoctrination objection aside, it remains worth noticing how the teaching of "information" and "factual knowledge" is typically denigrated in modern education as being somehow "second class" or not worthy of a serious teacher's efforts. More often than not, the teaching of information and factual knowledge is disparagingly predicated with the word "mere", as in "that's merely factual knowledge" or "mere information." Even Benjamin Bloom relegates this kind of learning to a low station in his taxonomy. But the thinking skills movement has been particularly disdainful of this kind of learning because it is viewed (either tacitly or overtly) as anathema to what their programs, which focus on the reasoning *process,* are all about. ("You don't want your kid to just know facts, do you?" God forbid!) However, our public understanding of what "information" and "factual knowledge" consist in have been conspicuously naive. Our operative notions of "information," "facts," and "factual knowledge" are not only among the most maligned concepts in education, but they are among the most poorly understood. We have not taken the time to understand or appreciate what is conceptually involved in "factual knowledge," nor how far it takes one toward the goal of autonomous thought.

Clearly, some types of information and factual knowledge are indeed educationally pointless or trivial. Perhaps learning a page of the encyclopedia (or phone book) by heart would be an example. Moreover, such examples are rhetorically cited, and thought of, by critics as paradigms of what is wrong with teaching facts or information in general. However, it is a serious mistake to regard the teaching and learning of factual information as educationally inferior. Most of the important things which our culture and mankind can be said to *know* are of a straightforward factual nature. The mistake that occurs in maligning factual teaching is that we tend to set up, or envisage, a false dichotomy between factual knowledge on the one hand and thinking on the other. We talk as though there were simple *facts,* which are relatively passive things (like *data*), and *thinking,* which is active; hence, the dichotomy. Bloom's taxonomy of educational objectives clearly supports this view, and Gilbert Ryle's

distinction between "knowing how" and "knowing that" has been interpreted by many educators as supporting it also.[3] No doubt this distinction
can sometimes be made, and it is often harmless to do so.

However, there have been, and continue to be, many disastrous consequences in education from reading far too much into this distinction. In
most of the interesting cases, and particularly those which are likely to
occur in school learning, the distinction between "knowing facts" and
"thinking" simply does not hold. Significant thought (i.e., thinking) is
required in coming to learn factual knowledge, and to use it. For example, that "osmotic pressure increases with the concentration of solution"
is a fact, and to understand this is to have *factual knowledge*. That $E =
MC^2$ is a fact, and to understand this is to have factual knowledge. Such
examples are clearly endless, and in each case the factual knowledge
requires thinking. That is, the factual knowledge *itself* requires thinking;
there are not two things going on in knowing facts, but one. This is
because *knowing* something logically entails understanding it—else we
would not say one "knows" it. And understanding requires thinking.
The thinking consists in (among other things) coming to see the fact or
proposition as part of a network of other facts or propositions which the
person already understands. There is an important sense in which people
cannot be said to know or understand isolated facts or propositions, but
only collections of them; because facts and propositions are composed
(logically) of other concepts, or facts, or propositions. Consider, for
example, even the relatively trivial piece of factual knowledge that
"Albany is the capital of New York." One must first understand what a
capital is, and that it is not necessarily the largest city, etc. The concept
of a "capital" is itself quasi-sophisticated. This is why second-grade
students do not understand the proposition "Albany is the capital of New
York," and why sixth graders do understand it. Similarly, sixth graders
do not understand the factual proposition about osmotic pressure (above),
and college sophomores do. In short, a lot of thinking, and sometimes
difficult thinking, is required in coming to understand factual information—at least the kind of information that schools have been traditionally
concerned to teach. Thus, it is a serious mistake to separate factual
knowledge, or information, from thinking. In reality, they cannot be
taken apart as easily as our educational talk (and theories) might suggest.
And I believe much positive harm is being done by continuing to talk
this way, as the "thinking skills" movement does.

Traditionally, initiation into the standard disciplines has never tried
to separate the thinking *process* from the information or facts to be
thought about. The disciplines have at least tacitly recognized that the
way one thinks about something is part of the warp and woof of what
is being thought *about:* mathematical questions require mathematical
thinking, moral problems, moral thinking, etc. And if some real "everyday" problem involves several of these dimensions (or facts) at once,

then several of these different learned dimensions will have to be employed to solve it. There is no getting around this brute fact of intellectual life. Thus, the pedagogical task which lies before our educational institutions is to get on with the business of teaching the disciplines in the most enlightened ways that we know. No available alternative can even come close to producing critical thinkers of the sort we all desire.

CHAPTER 4

Some practical guidelines for teaching critical thinking

I defend the view that the standard disciplines already contain the necessary cognitive ingredients for critical thinking. However, many a frustrated high school or college teacher (not to mention the public) will object that the disciplines are not, in fact, producing critical thinkers, nor indeed noticeably *autonomous* thinkers. The objection is, in effect, that if the disciplines are so efficacious, why are we not seeing more evidence of critical or autonomous thought from contemporary students? Let me confess I share this grim assessment of the present situation in secondary schools, and beyond. Whether the criticism refers to disciplinary thinking or critical thinking *per se*, there is far less autonomous thinking (of any kind) than we are entitled to expect. However, confronted with this situation as we are, we must ask a basic question: is this dismal state of affairs the result of some inherent deficiency in the disciplines for producing critical thinkers, or does it have more to do with the ways in which these subjects are contingently taught? I think the latter is the case. At least part of the problem begins with many teachers' own conception of their discipline. They do not see clearly enough the purpose, structure, and potential of their own subject; so, naturally, much of this becomes lost for the student as well. Most disciplines contain large bodies of knowledge and information, and various methods for exploring experience. But it will not do to simply tap into this body of knowledge anywhere that the teachers' interest strikes them. Not all knowledge about plants, for example, is equally rich or useful, and not all historical events are equally capable of conveying a sense of the past.

Most disciplines have certain key concepts and ideas which are more fundamental than the rest; and they are more fundamental because they are the most powerful ideas in the sense that they take in a broader sweep of experience. These key concepts and ideas of the disciplines are the basic building blocks for intelligently talking about and exploring experience. The remaining knowledge and understanding in the discipline derives from them, not *vice versa*. Some of you will recognize that I am here referring to Jerome Bruner's notion of the "structure of disciplines." Indeed I am. I completely agree with him as to what content should constitute the curriculum; and that this can be viewed as a "spiral curriculum" as one proceeds through the years of study.[1] However, I differ from Bruner (and Piaget for that matter) regarding the importance of language and linguistic competence. For me, linguistic (or symbolic) competence accounts for most of the variance in understanding something, particularly a discipline. Bruner is interested in, and talks a great deal about, what he calls "intuitive thinking" and various "skills," which are nonlinguistic in character. At one point, in fact, Bruner contrasts the "articulate idiot" in a subject with the "inarticulate genius." But to me, the notion of an "articulate idiot" is very close to a contradiction in terms, almost like the notion of a "brave coward." Moreover, Bruner's most famous dictum is that "any subject can be taught effectively in some intellectually honest form to any child at any stage of development." He views the pedagogical problem to be largely one of "translation" of concepts to the child's level. However, we should notice that this problem of "translation" can very often be one enormous problem precisely because much of the difficulty in higher learning consists in coming to grips with its complex and powerful terms—terms which are used to express sophisticated ideas. The term *neutrino* for example, is simple enough—it describes a subatomic particle. But to fully understand that term, and to be able to use it effectively, requires knowing a lot of physics. This is precisely why young children cannot normally do physics: it requires a long and somewhat arduous period of nurturing into its conceptual framework.

Thus, while I differ with Bruner on his lack of emphasis on language (or linguistic competence), I agree entirely with the need to teach the structure of disciplines. And I agree with him for the same reasons that he provides, namely, that the broad concepts and principles which codify a discipline come closer than any available alternative to solving the problem of *transfer* of learning. (This problem, by the way, remains a particularly serious problem for so-called "thinking skills" programs.) Bruner describes how transfer is connected to structured content as follows:

> In essence, it consists of learning initially not a skill but a general idea, which can then be used as a basis for recognizing subsequent problems as special cases of the idea originally mastered. This type of transfer is at the heart of the educational process—the continual broadening and deepening of knowledge in terms of basic and general ideas. The continuity of learning that is produced by the transfer of principles is dependent upon mastery of the structure of the subject matter . . . that is to say, in order for a person to be able to recognize the applicability of an idea to a new situation and to broaden his learning thereby, he must have clearly in mind the general nature of the phenomenon with which he is dealing. (*The Process of Education*, pp. 17–18)

Moreover, there have been at least fifty empirical studies conducted since the mid-seventies which confirm this Brunerian view that *reasoning skill*, and the useful *transfer* of it, are domain-specific.[2]

Even Robert Sternberg, who, ironically, has now become associated with the thinking skills movement, says:

> In our studies, high-aptitude individuals appear to be skillful reasoners because of the level of their content knowledge as well as because of their knowledge of the procedural constraints of a particular problem form . . . Learning and reasoning skills develop not as abstract mechanisms of heuristic search and memory processing. Rather, they develop as the content and concepts of a knowledge domain are attained in learning situations that constrain this knowledge to serve certain purposes and goals . . . As this knowledge is used and transferred to domains of related knowledge, the skills involved probably then become more generalizable so that intelligent performance is displayed in the context of novel ("nonentrenched") situations. ("Intelligence and Nonentrenchment," *Journal of Educational Psychology* 73 [1981] 1–16)

In short: what Wittgenstein had observed from a *philosophical* point of view, and what Bruner had argued from a *curriculum* point of view, is now overwhelmingly supported by the available *empirical evidence;* namely, that reasoning is not a generalized detachable skill, but is connected to domains of content, notably the standard disciplines. Teachers are more than entitled, therefore, to have renewed faith in the potential of their disciplines, to be "born again" if you like, and should not feel the least bit guilty for allowing the "thinking skills revolution" to pass them by.

However, the first thing teachers must do is to get a clearer fix on the structure of their discipline, and to use that as the core of their curriculum. There is, moreover, a large and interesting literature already available to assist teachers in doing this.[4]

In addition to being clear about *what* one is trying to teach, there remains the question of *how* one should teach the structure of a discipline. It is here, I believe, that the major failing of the disciplines is to be found. Even in those cases where the structure of the discipline has been the core of the curriculum, the method of delivery has been anathema to critical thinking. The didactic method of teaching and the receptive method of learning have simply been carried over to secondary school from grade school. But secondary school is the place to shift gears; what was necessary in the early years is no longer so. Here is the place to nurture discussion, argument, and the free exchange of ideas within a subject. While the disciplines should remain the focus of study, discussion and argument should be the major means of teaching and learning. Not only do discussion and argument enable students to understand the disciplines more deeply, in an epistemological sense, but they enable students to partake in autonomous discourse about these things. It helps to provide those characteristics in students which, we all agree, are desirable: those characteristics which many people regard as tantamount to critical thinking.

The problem has been that secondary school teaching and learning has simply been an extension of what takes place in grade school. It is just more of the same, with slightly longer assignments. The *Encyclopedia Britannica* continues to be the major resource for term papers, except students now paraphrase instead of directly copying. The reason that the disciplines have not been producing autonomous or critical thinkers is that we have never seriously tried it! Wanting it and actually trying it are two different things. If students are required to discuss and argue for things, they will quickly learn to do it. Students are not fools; they do what is expected of them. If regurgitation and getting the "right" answer are what bring high marks, then that is what they will try to do. If original discussion and argument are clearly expected of them, then they will do that. I am sure that there is a causal connection between what students do and what you expect of them. Indeed, this is almost a tautology. However, autonomous and critical thinking has not been clearly woven into the fabric of our curriculum; hence, it is not surprising that we are seeing little evidence of it.

Several obstacles have stood in the way of having critical thinking be a more visible part of disciplinary thinking. But all of these are surmountable. One such obstacle, which must be faced, is the simple fact that some subjects, such as mathematics, are not quite so readily amenable to autonomous or critical thinking. In some subjects, that is, we are simply (and appropriately) trying to *train* students "how to do it." Thus, there is little room for critical thinking in some cases. This is not to say that these subjects do not allow critical thought, but simply that it is not the appropriate focus. Typing classes might be another example here—critical thinking, as such, might even get in the way.

There is more than ample room, however, for autonomous and critical thinking in science, history, literature, and the social studies. But if tests and class performance simply require a student to memorize these subjects, then you can bet that is what you will get, even here. Students study subjects in the way that they will be tested on them. If you typically ask questions like "What did X say about Y?" or "When did X happen?" or "Why does this reaction occur?" then students memorize. If, on the other hand, you ask questions like "What are X's reasons for believing Y, and do you think he is right? If not, why not?" then a student *must,* perforce, engage in autonomous thought. Such questions are shot through with autonomous thinking, it cannot be avoided. And if students do not produce this kind of thinking, then you simply fail them. They must come to see that having their own thoughts about things is the name of the game in school. And we must have the courage to enforce it. It is both hypocritical and confusing to students to not assess them for precisely what you are trying to teach them. If you want critical thinking, then you must ask questions that require it, and assess them accordingly. They will quickly get the message.

Courses in literary criticism and philosophy courses, to name just two, have been requiring this kind of thinking for generations. I see no endemic reasons why most secondary school courses cannot be taught this way as well. Science and history are no less open to critical questioning than are literary criticism and philosophy. But teachers must be prepared to assess the *quality* of the students' reasoning and articulation every bit as much as they have been prepared to mark the "right" answers in the past. Pedagogically comfortable questions which have single "right" answers have to be replaced with questions which don't have them. If we are not ready to do this, then we are not ready to teach critical thinking, and we have to stop blaming the students. Again, students do what they are required to do.

There is also a more subtle and more difficult obstacle to nurturing critical thinking in the classroom, which stems from the teacher's attitude or mode of conducting discussion. True critical or autonomous thinking is, by definition, doing *one's own* thinking; therefore, students must be cut loose from their dependency on authority. Yet teachers in a classroom are in a *de facto* position of authority, and this fact has a deleterious effect upon the free and open exchange of ideas. It can be like having an adult referee at a teenage pillow fight. Thus, the pedagogical problem is one of conveying the idea that reason and argument are the only acceptable currency in the pursuit of truth, and that even the teacher's views must be subjected to this tribunal. But students are not likely to push for reasons so long as they feel dominated by the authority of teachers and textbooks. The teacher, therefore, must find ways to put his/her authority open to critical examination, and the same for textbooks.

The critical examination of ideas can be nurtured by teachers in a variety of ways; one of the more effective is to engage students in argument. Perhaps the most refreshing—indeed, the most liberating—thing about honest argument is that it requires taking the other person's reasons seriously, no matter how bizarre they might seem, and addressing them head-on. In argument, notice, people have to treat each other as equals. Thus, in the arena of argument even the teacher's traditional authority must give way to reasons. This is precisely the kind of thinking and discussion that the schools should be trying to foster. The attitude of the teacher and the intellectual atmosphere of the class have to instill confidence in students that rational disagreement will not be penalized in any way, but highly rewarded. A teacher can say, for example, either in discussion or in comments on an essay, things like "I find your arguments on this unconvincing because you fail to consider X or Y, but it is at least plausible, and you gave the thesis a good run for its money—mark: A." Students will come to see that agreement with the teacher is not necessary for high marks, but autonomous thinking is.

Again, student essays in literature and philosophy have been routinely marked this way. This simply needs to be brought into the open and emphasized in every subject across the curriculum. With this done, we will have accomplished what we have been trying to do. Against this kind of background, drills and training in specific "thinking skills," as such, can be seen as either superfluous or redundant: such skills are an integral part of disciplinary thinking.

Finally, a word about the grass-roots practicality of this proposal. Some people have been tempted to argue that it is easier said than done, and that teachers are not in fact up to the task of teaching the disciplines in a more discursive or argumentative way. Thus, the argument runs, it is better to introduce "thinking skills" or "argument analysis" into the training of teachers (and college students) as the best way to address the present deficiencies. However, setting aside the arguments about the lack of cognitive transfer of "thinking skills," these solutions are actually more labor-intensive for both students and institutions. Most teachers and college students have never had a course in analytic philosophy, and even fewer have had a course in logic or argument analysis. To become proficient in these logical and analytical skills requires mastery of an entirely new set of concepts and procedures—something which requires intensive study and extensive practice. It is, in effect, to learn a new discipline; and nothing short of this can adequately prepare teachers to teach logic. Those who think these skills can be mastered in a simple summer workshop are kidding themselves. I have been teaching philosophy and logic (at all levels) long enough to believe otherwise. To have these analytical thinking skills become functionally usable requires vigilance and time. Add to this, that secondary school teachers must learn to apply these skills in specific subject areas which are quite different from those in a logic class. These are not trivial problems; and they cannot be negated by simple enthusiasm for a particular thinking skills program.

I have already discussed some of the difficulties facing a rejuvenated disciplinary approach to critical thinking; and, by contrast, they are not nearly so formidable as the "thinking skills" approach. To begin with, teachers do not have to learn any new subject matter, new concepts, or new skills. Rather, they can remain on the familiar turf of their subject area, where they already have most confidence. All that is required are two comparatively simple shifts of emphasis: (1) to learn, or to improve, their methods for teaching the "structure of the discipline", and (2) to change their method of presentation from a didactic mode to a more discursive or argumentative mode of teaching and assessment. These two changes, all by themselves, could equip students with a powerful set of cultural lenses, and the wherewithal to discuss them intelligently. Thus, setting aside the theoretical case for the disciplinary approach, and the empirical evidence supporting it, I would argue that the *practicalities* of implementation favor this approach as well. All it needs is better PR to help it overcome the gadgetry of so-called thinking skills.

CHAPTER 5

Problems of evaluating critical thinking programs

For the past few years I have defended a view about the nature of critical thinking (and how to teach it) that runs counter to the dominant view in North America.[1] I have argued that the major ingredient of critical thinking is context-specific, field-dependent *knowledge* and *information*. And, contrary to the received opinion, critical thinking has little (if anything) to do with so-called general reasoning skills or the like. My view of critical thinking, moreover, has led me to reject courses in informal logic, and to advocate approaches to critical thinking which attempt to increase one's capacity for understanding complex concepts, information, and problems—as the traditional disciplines try to do. Thus, the differences between the standard approach and my own view are twofold: we disagree over both the ingredients of critical thinking and how to teach it.

One of the recurrent criticisms leveled against my view is the charge that I am advancing an empirical thesis without presenting data.[2] For example, Robert Ennis, in rebutting my rejection of informal logic and critical thinking courses, says, "He has offered no empirical evidence on this matter," and concludes quite unequivocally, "I think that the basic issue is now an empirical one and should be dealt with empirically."[3] While I have always thought this claim at the very least to be tendentious, I have subsequently discovered quite a few studies which share the same belief that the evaluation of critical thinking programs is essentially an empirical question.[4] It is this claim, then, which provides the motivation and central focus of the present essay. If I cannot get you to share my skepticism about empirically evaluating critical thinking, I hope to at least expose for you some of the serious difficulties that confront such an evaluation.

Burden of proof

There is a long and respected tradition in philosophy which requires that when someone makes an existence claim, be it for a God, a ghost, or a unicorn, the burden of proof is on the person making the existence claim to justify the belief—the onus is not on the doubter to disprove it. This tradition should extend to the evaluation of critical thinking programs. When test-and-measurement enthusiasts talk about *measuring* such things as "critical reasoning ability" or "general reasoning skills," the onus is on them to be very clear about what they mean by these terms, and to prove that such "general abilities" really exist. Certainly, if someone claimed to be measuring a person's ESP power with an electroencephalograph, for example, we would be properly skeptical about just what was meant by "ESP," and how it was known that ESP was being measured. In both cases, the onus is on the measurer to make the case, not on the doubter to disprove it.

Elsewhere I have argued that the very conception of a "general reasoning ability," or the like, is conceptually incoherent. It is incoherent in the same way that, say, being "generally speedy" is incoherent. That is, we do not posit a single skill called "speed" or "general speediness" to an individual because we properly realize that there are just too many different ways that a person can be slow or speedy (e.g., running, typing, or changing mufflers). No one, to my knowledge, has ever established that there exists anything which might legitimately be called "critical thinking ability" or "general reasoning skill." Even the giants of psychology and psychometrics have come up empty-handed. For example, J. P. Guildford, in his paper entitled "The Nature of the General Reasoning Factor," concludes that:

> a common unique, psychological core for all problem solving does not exist. Problems are simply too varied, and each type seems to call upon its own pattern of abilities—perceptual abilities as well as thinking abilities . . . In conclusion, we may say that it has been much easier to decide what *general reasoning* is not than to say what it is.[5]

In a very recent and lengthy review of the psychological literature on deductive reasoning, published in 1982, Jonathan Evans reports that:

> From consideration of the material reviewed in parts I to III of this book, it appears that there is little evidence for the influence of a general system of logical competence, and that the thought processes involved are highly *content-dependent*.

Later, he adds:

> We are forced to the conclusion that people manifest little ability for general deductive reasoning in these experiments. Very little behavior can be attributed to an *a priori* system that is independent of the particular task content and structure. This does not mean that people cannot reason correctly in contexts where they have no relevant and appropriate experience—indeed some evidence suggests that they can. It does mean, however, that adults' reasoning ability is far more concrete and context-dependent than has been generally believed.[6]

And David Ausubel, after a lengthy analysis of the research on psychological transfer, concludes straight off:

> Hence critical thinking cannot be taught as a generalized ability. In practice it can be enhanced only by adopting a precise, logical, analytic, and critical approach to the teaching of a particular discipline, an approach that fosters appreciation of scientific method in that discipline. Also, from a purely theoretical standpoint alone, it hardly seems plausible that a strategy of inquiry that must necessarily be broad enough to be applicable to a wide range of disciplines and problems can ever have, at the same time, sufficient *particular* relevance to be helpful in the solution of the *specific* problem at hand.[7]

Likewise, Gagne rejects the transfer of general abilities of this new type also, as did Thorndike thirty-five years before him when he decisively discredited "faculty psychology" and the "mental discipline" approach to education. Save for IQ, I know of no reputable psychometric researcher who supports the existence of something which might properly be termed "general reasoning ability" or "critical thinking ability." Thus, considered as a general ability, the burden of proof remains, as it does with ESP and UFOs, on the shoulders of the proponents of "critical thinking ability." In the meantime, serious skepticism is surely justified.

Alternatively, when critical thinking is considered as some *set* of abilities, such as those described in the Watson and Glaser test, or in Robert Ennis's "general aspects," the situation is not measurably improved. All the tests which purport to measure these "abilities" do two things:

(1) they merely *assume* that the phenomena being tested are in fact *useful to* or *productive of* real critical thinking (i.e., that the tests have external validity); and,

(2) because the tests postulate certain singular, requisite "abilities" (e.g., "the ability to evaluate evidence," "the ability to recognize underlying assumptions"), it is then *assumed* that there *exist* such unitary underlying abilities corresponding to these descriptions.

In the first instance they are *assuming* what needs to be proven (known to fallacy buffs as "begging the question"); and in the second instance they are *reifying the existence* of a pervasive "ability" from its description. Harold Berlak, for example, was absolutely correct in criticizing Robert Ennis's "general aspects" for merely assuming their usefulness. He says:

> The value of any set of intellectual skills (Ennis calls them aspects) rests on whether they have demonstrated value to persons who have dealt successfully with some problem or issue. This is the "ultimate" test of any set of intellectual operations . . . [At] some point it must be shown that the aspects selected are

of major importance to persons who are attempting to deal with issues or problems. Certainly, if a reading expert proposed that knowledge of certain aspects of linguistics is important to the learning of reading, we would expect the proposition to be defended by argument and, if possible, with data. Similarly, if knowledge of the aspects of thinking selected by Ennis or anyone else is of major importance to the process of engaging in critical discourse, then we should expect a justification for selection in terms of argument and data. Ennis does not do this, and rarely does anyone else. In most of the writings in the area, the value of operations is assumed to be prima facie.[8]

Moreover, these same *assumed* "aspects" by Ennis are what the Cornell Critical Thinking Tests (Levels X and Z) purport to be measuring. (Note: Ennis is the major author of the Cornell tests.)

The widely used *Watson-Glaser Critical Thinking Appraisal* purports to measure five distinct "abilities." Let us look at the sole justification provided for the belief that five unitary abilities underlie critical thinking.

Dressel and Mayhew (1954) have listed the following abilities that appear to be related to the concept of critical thinking:

- The ability to define a problem
- The ability to select pertinent information for the solution of a problem
- The ability to recognize stated and unstated assumptions
- The ability to formulate and select relevant and promising hypotheses
- The ability to draw valid conclusions and judge the validity of inferences

Judgments of qualified persons and results of research studies (Houle, 1943; Morse & McCune, 1957) support the author's belief that the items in the *Critical Thinking Appraisal* represent an adequate sample of the above five abilities and that the total score yielded by the test represents a valid estimate of the proficiency of individuals with respect to these aspects of critical thinking.[9]

Here you have it. How do Watson and Glaser know that there are true "abilities" at work here? Answer: because they took them from a list provided by Dressel and Mayhew in a government document. But how do Dressel and Mayhew know that there are "abilities" corresponding to these descriptions? Answer: because they "*appear* to be related to the concept of critical thinking." Thus, we have one person's "appearance" serving as the next person's "reality," which has subsequently served as the basis of hundreds of "empirical" studies in the area.

We have here in microcosm the chronology of how a casual phrase ("critical thinking abilities") can become a recurrent piece of educational jargon, which is eventually *reified* into a cognitive ability—in this case, a latent trait.

Specifically, what I think has gone wrong in this instance is that educators and measurement-types have mistakenly taken the description of an achievement as indicative of an ability. Notice, for example, that such things as "defining a problem" or "recognizing underlying assumptions," or "correctly evaluating evidence" are all descriptions of *achievements*—in each case something has been successfully accomplished. Notice further that achievements do not necessarily *describe* corresponding abilities. For example, the statements "He reached the summit of the mountain" and "He crossed the finish line" both describe achievements, but in neither case do you know *how* it was done. The summit could have been reached by helicopter, or the finish line could have been sailed across, walked across, or driven across. In neither case do we know what actual "abilities" were involved in the achievement. Similarly, for such achievements as "defining a problem" or "correctly evaluating evidence," one cannot assume that a unitary "ability" is indicated, nor be certain what that "ability" might be like. In such cases, literally hundreds of separate abilities might have been involved, or, conversely, nothing recognizable as an ability might have been involved. Thus, despite the prevalent jargon, there are insufficient grounds for believing either that such abilities actually exist, or that standardized tests are measuring them. To repeat, the burden of proof remains with the claimant in this case, not with the skeptic.

The definition of "critical thinking" and empiricism

Yet another obstacle in the path of measuring the effectiveness of various critical thinking programs is that different *definitions* of "critical thinking" will require different criteria of measurement. That is, for different meanings of "critical thinking," different kinds of behavior will count as evidence for it. Thus, tests of critical thinking are not empirically neutral, but are decidedly theory-laden with their own specific notions of "critical thinking." When Robert Ennis and others assert that "the issue is now an empirical one and should be dealt with empirically,"[10] it's not at all clear how this can be fairly done. Where there are competing conceptions of critical thinking, it is unlikely that any neutral test can arbitrate among them.

Indeed, the evaluation of critical thinking programs is not unlike the difficulty of evaluating "therapy" for some neurosis in psychiatry. The problem is exacerbated when you have therapists from different theoretical orientations. For example, a Freudian and a radical behaviorist cannot even agree on the *type* of evidence which should count as relevant to such an evaluation. The Freudian is likely to require only that the patient integrate the neurotic behavior into his personality so that he is no longer troubled or uncomfortable with the problem. Thus, when trauma and discord have been reduced, and psychic harmony has been achieved, the Freudian declares the therapy a "success." The radical behaviorist, on the other hand, is not concerned with how the neurotic *feels,* but is interested only in what he or she *does*. For the behaviorist, therapy is successful when, and only when, the overt behavior stops. On this view, the patient's oral reports of harmony or discord are quite beside the point. Thus, these different conceptions of a "cure" require correspondingly different kinds of evidence to support them; there is no neutral test for a cure that can decide between these therapeutic orientations. Thus, it is not at all clear that we are dealing with an empirical question here, since neither side accepts the other's "evidence" as evidence.

The standard conception of an empirical question is: "that which is decidable by appealing to objective experience." But in this case, what kind of experience should count as objective experience? This question, notice, is not itself an empirical question, yet it lies at the heart of the dispute between our two competing therapists. It follows from these considerations that the original question "*Which* therapeutic method is most effective?" is not in fact an empirical question. The reason that it is not an empirical question is because there is a distinctly *normative* (i.e., valuational) component to the conception of "cure." And normative questions are neither true nor false, but more related to such things as approval or disapproval, and likes or dislikes. For similar reasons, then, my dispute with Ennis and standard courses in critical thinking is not just an empirical issue. It is not just an empirical issue because we have different conceptions of what critical thinking is, and therefore different standards for admissible evidence.

To be perhaps excessively brief about it, the major differences between Ennis's view (which I take to be the standard view) and my own might be summarized as follows. Ennis's definition of critical thinking is "the correct assessment of statements," and he believes the proper training for this consists in what might normally be included in an informal logic course. Also, evidence for the successful achievement of the relevant skills can be measured by performance on standardized tests such as the Cornell Critical Thinking Tests or the Watson-Glaser test. These are the major features of the standard view. In my view, by contrast, critical thinking has little or nothing to do with performance on these standardized tests because, for me, critical thinking has to do with "engaging in an activity with reflective skepticism," and there are almost as many ways of doing this as there are kinds of activities. For me, there is no enumerable set of skills which demarcates critical thinking, so no single test could ever hope to capture it. Moreover, the normative difference between the standard approach to critical thinking and my own is that the standard approach takes its criteria for *good performance* from the field of informal logic, whereas I take my criteria from the different fields of study and activity. For these reasons then, the dispute between the standard approach (e.g., Ennis *et al.*) and my own view is not an empirical issue: we do not agree on the definition of "critical thinking," nor on the criteria for judging good performance, nor even on what constitutes evidence for critical thinking. This latter point is of sufficient interest and importance to warrant separate treatment here.

The conflation of "empiricism" with tests and measurement

En route to charging me with having made an empirical claim without substantiation, Ennis cites a study by David and Linda Annis, "Does Philosophy Improve Critical Thinking?",[11] as an example of the general type of evidence needed not only to settle the dispute between him and myself, but to establish the effectiveness of critical thinking programs generally. Briefly, the Annis study is a typical statistical analysis of *pre*- and *post*-test results for different groups of students undergoing different course treatments. That is, it attempts to measure quantitatively the "impact" of several undergraduate courses on critical thinking ability. However, quite apart from any of the study's results, which were paltry, the study is of interest because it is an excellent example of some confusions which underlie much of the educational evaluation literature in general and the critical thinking evaluation literature in particular.

The confusions I have in mind are twofold. They tend to occur together in practice, so I will try to separate them here for purposes of analysis. Both confusions, however, stem from a rather virulent form of instrumentalism, or a desire for test standardization, where the measurement tail wags the educational dog. The first such confusion is the tendency to equate "empiricism" with tests and statistical measurement—the assumption that for something to be "empirically known" it must be test-measurable. As Elliot Eisner observed:

> Becoming familiar with correlation procedures too often leads simply to questions about what one can correlate: the existence of statistically reliable achievement too often leads to a conception of achievement that is educationally eviscerated. Our tools, as useful as they might be initially, often become our masters, indeed what it means to do any type of research at all in education is defined, stamped, sealed and approved by utilizing particular premises and procedures. A brief excursion into the pages of the *American Educational Research Journal* will provide living testimony to the range of such premises and procedures. For example, during the past three volume years the AERJ has published over 100 articles. Of these only three were nonstatistical in character.[12]

In the Annis paper "Does Philosophy Improve Critical Thinking?" the authors strongly intimate that if you cannot statistically measure the effects of your courses, then your belief in their value rests on dogmatism. In response to a statement by Bertrand Russell, touting the educational virtues of philosophy, the Annises say:

Although we may believe that philosophy has such an impact on our students, what evidence do we have for this belief? It is noteworthy that philosophers are quick to criticize others for unsupported views, but when it comes to the issue of why philosophy is valuable, we ourselves rely on dogma . . . A measure of the impact of philosophy on critical reasoning would be a comparison of the amount of improvement on the Watson-Glaser between philosophy and the control group. If the difference in the improvement on the total score is statistically significant, that is, if there is a low probability that the difference is due to chance alone, then we may conclude there is a differential impact. The statistical technique of analysis of variance is a measure of this differential impact. Analysis of variance applied to the subtests of the Watson-Glaser provides information on the specific impact of philosophy and the various courses.[13]

It is clear the Annises think that Russell's faith in the value of philosophy borders on dogmatism, since he never statistically measured its effects with standardized instruments such as they recommend. Indeed, throughout the Annis study it is assumed that the value of any course of study cannot be known unless it is test-measured. No other type of evidence will seem to do.

It is arguable, however, that the Annises' unflinching reliance on such psychometric procedures is equally "dogmatic" since, as in this case, the validity of the testing instrument (i.e., Watson-Glaser) and the soundness of the research design are usually open to serious challenge.[14] One is here reminded of G. E. Moore's proof of the external world where, holding his hand up in front of him, he declared, "This is a hand before me"; and this, he argued, is more certain than any principle of skepticism upon which one's doubt might be based. In the social sciences, as in daily life, it is likely that there are more phenomena which *resist* accurate and valid measurement than there are those which submit to it; and it is always open to question which kind of phenomenon one has before one. Thus, as in Moore's argument, there is often as much reason to question indirect statistical evidence about the efficacy of critical thinking programs, or educational programs, as there is to accept one's own evidence based on direct inspection.

I would like to make it clear that I am not opposed to the broad use of statistical research procedures in education, and I would be among the first to defend their usefulness in many situations. However, I would suggest that when they are used to assess programs which are intended to have wide-ranging outcomes, such as a liberal education program, or a critical thinking program, they pose very serious validity problems. So much so that there is more reason to question their validity (as in Moore's proof) than there is to accept their validity at face value. In the Annis study, for example, the entire second half of the paper is spent offering methodological alibis for why they failed to find any statistically significant results in this study. They say: maybe we should have taught them longer, maybe we should have more items in the subscales, maybe we should have tried the Cornell, maybe we didn't teach the philosophy correctly that we did teach, etc. It never occurs to the Annises that maybe, like measuring sweetness with a yardstick, there is something wrong-headed in what they were trying to do, that there is a bad fit between what they want to know and how they are trying to find out. It is no accident that complex courses or programs which are intended to have diverse outcomes, are not normally evaluated psychometrically, let alone in a pre-test/post-test format. We seem to realize intuitively that our methods of direct inspection of these programs are usually more valid than psychometric test instruments. To demand statistical rigor where it is not likely to be forthcoming is an instance of what A. N. Whitehead called "the fallacy of misplaced concreteness." We should not feel lacking in academic "integrity," as the Annises actually suggest at one point, because we do not share their enthusiasm for the psychometric evaluation of critical thinking programs. Rather, we should be acutely aware, as they are not, of the very real limitations of these procedures.

A second confusion pervading the Annis study is the assumption that the sole purpose of education is to develop skills, as such, which have *instrumental* value; moreover, these skills are always considered to be psychometrically test-measurable. There is a total failure to recognize that much of our educational knowledge and understanding does not involve skills of any kind, yet it has an *intrinsic* value to us. That the Annises value the various educational subject areas solely in terms of their instrumental value can be seen from the fact that on every page of their article there is at least one reference to the "impact" which subject area X has on critical thinking. Indeed, the noun *impact* is the single most recurrent word in the paper. It is clear that for them subjects are not studied for their own power and interest, but rather for what impact these subjects make upon critical thinking ability *per se*. Here is a sample of the Annises' instrumental interpretation of educational value:

> Although we may believe that philosophy has such an *impact* on our students, what evidence do we have for this belief? It is noteworthy that philosophers are quick to criticize others for unsupported views, but when it comes to the issue of why philosophy is valuable, we ourselves rely on dogma. The same principles of rational belief that commit philosophers to the careful and critical assessment of the reasons for some philosophical views, require us to be concerned with empirical support for claims made about the *impact* philosophy has on students. The present study is an initial step at empirically assessing the claim that the study of philosophy improves a person's ability to think critically. (P. 145, italics mine)

Elsewhere:

At present, however, there is practically no direct empirical evidence of what *impact,* if any, philosophy has. Furthermore, even if philosophy does have an *impact,* we need to know more specifically what effects it has . . . What specific abilities are affected by these courses? Since we do not know what *impact* philosophy has, we also are ignorant of instructional factors affecting critical thinking in philosophy. (P. 147, italics mine)

The Annises never even entertain the possibility that the value and purpose of philosophy does not reside in its capacity to "impact" (the new verb) skills or abilities as such, but that, rather, to do philosophy just is to engage in critical thought. That is what the discipline *is.* Philosophy does not try to develop instrumental skills as such, but rather to provide insight and understanding about the frailty of the human condition. Having this insight and understanding just is to be thinking critically. Herein lies its power and its purpose; its purpose is not to develop skills, such as those the Annises want to test for. The purpose and value of philosophy, as with most academic disciplines, is to provide a perspective through knowledge and understanding. And this perspective, I would argue, is the most important ingredient in any situation requiring critical thinking.

The Annises' emphasis upon skills, and their consequent deemphasis of knowledge and understanding as provided by the traditional disciplines, is symptomatic of a wider trend in the critical thinking literature. This literature all but ignores the traditional liberal arts disciplines, or dismisses them as though they were irrelevant relics in an academic museum. The disciplines, the thinking goes, exist merely for the enjoyment of academic specialists, and a few artsy eccentrics. In critical thinking textbooks, the power of liberal arts education has been either brushed aside or forgotten in a kind of mass amnesia suggestive of a new dark age. This represents either a loss of faith or a failure to remember that the origin and justification of the liberal arts has always been that it liberates people from everyday ignorance. Moreover, it liberates people from ignorance about everyday problems. That is, it does so in precisely those situations that the so-called critical thinking skills purport to be so useful. It seems we need to be reminded that history, literature, philosophy, and science *are about this everyday world.* They are not museum pieces, but rather they provide the perspective from which rational beliefs and decisions are made, and from which they can be judged. Indeed, Paul Hirst argues that to use these traditional forms of thought is synonymous with having a rational mind. If this view is even partially correct, then it has already demonstrated its centrality to situations requiring critical thought. For these reasons, I favor improving our methods for teaching the disciplines in trying to develop critical thinkers. Whichever way one resolves this pedagogic issue, however, I hope I have made it clear that the question about evaluating critical thinking programs is anything but a straightforward empirical one.

PART II

Critiques of the position

CHAPTER 6

Thinking about critical thinking: philosophers can't go it alone

Stephen P. Norris

In reviewing a paper of mine which was a philosophical analysis of some aspects of test validation theory, the reviewer began with a disclaimer:

> Although an undergraduate philosophy minor, and although explicitly trained in graduate school in a logical empiricist tradition, I am not a philosopher and make no such pretense. This is partly atrophy and partly deliberate choice; I have long felt that philosophers worry too much about differences that don't matter.

As I read the review, I was reminded of C. P. Snow writing twenty-five years ago about the two cultures, the sciences and the humanities: "Thirty years ago the cultures had long ceased to speak to each other: but at least they managed a kind of frozen smile across the gulf. Now the politeness has gone, and they just make faces." The reviewer was not polite in my estimation in dismissing a whole school of disciplined thought, nor correct in saying that philosophers deal with issues that do not matter, but the attitude implied in the reviewer's remarks is one which is often displayed.

Philosophers are guilty of similar behavior. For example, many philosophers have been in the habit of pronouncing on how science ought to be done without ever actually getting their hands dirty doing science. The closest they get to science is the reading of research reports, which of course are substantially streamlined versions of what takes place. More germane to the present topic is the fact that philosophers often pronounce on issues related to critical thinking without due regard to the relevance of existing scientific research, or even to the fact that scientific results could *conceivably* matter. In this paper I propose to examine three questions related to thinking about critical thinking, and while acknowledging the relevance of philosophical considerations show they are insufficient by themselves for providing complete answers to the questions. The three questions are: (1) How should "critical thinking" be defined? (2) Is critical thinking ability generalizable across subject matter areas? And (3) How ought the validity of critical thinking tests be determined?

The definition of "critical thinking"

It has been a common practice for philosophers to provide what are called "conceptual analyses" of key concepts of education, psychology, and other disciplines. Ryle's concept of mind[1] and Peters's concept of motivation[2] are two examples of this type of work. In our own field we are well aware of the many attempts to provide a conceptual analysis of *education, teaching, learning,* and other concepts central to schooling and education. In a similar fashion, there have been attempts to provide conceptions of good thinking. In the field of critical thinking, one of the most widely-known attempts to do this is Robert Ennis's attempt[3] to provide a comprehensive set of criteria for determining when someone is a critical thinker. The type of definition he has provided has been called "programmatic"[4] because it recommends the adoption of a program or a point of view, or "reforming"[5] because it outlines a precise meaning for an expression with favorable connotations but no commonly accepted precise meaning.

Indeed, Ennis's view is both programmatic and reforming in the senses above. If we examine only his conception of deductive logical competence, which constitutes but one aspect of his larger view of critical thinking competence, he is seen arguing that the broad conception he offers, although inclusive of elements which many people might not call logic, is more useful for educational purposes than a narrower conception.[6] We are thus urged to adopt his view of deductive competence, and presumably of critical thinking competence in general, because of its conceptual soundness and usefulness to education.

John McPeck sees this approach of Ennis's to be based upon "a naive form of logical positivism."[7] Defining critical thinking by listing criteria for applying the expression is straightforward operationalism on McPeck's view. Ennis would probably not be persuaded by McPeck's objection and would probably wonder why he could not give definitions in this way, especially since the expression being defined is in dire need of clarification.

The point I wish to make is that this issue of the definition of critical thinking is not likely to be resolvable with the information that is currently available, and with the approach being followed by Ennis and McPeck. To see what sorts of additional information are needed, we first need to understand what is claimed when it is said that someone has critical thinking ability. Ability claims such as this are in my estimation[8] categorical claims about people's either genetically or environmentally determined natures. Specifically, to say that someone has critical thinking ability is to make a claim about a mental power which that person possesses. Mental powers, in turn, arise from mental structures and processes in the same way that physical powers (magnetism is an example) arise from the internal structures and processes of physical objects.

If abilities are understood in this way, then how is the task of defining an ability such as critical thinking ability to be understood? As a first step, I submit, a claim is made at a *generic* level of existence of *some* mental ability, a claim based on the observable behaviors of people. People do certain things—they perform deductive proofs, they appraise observation statements, they devise best explanations of phenomena, and they adjudicate disputes over value—and we rightly ascribe to them mental capacity for doing these things. At this initial stage, however, this ascription must be at the generic level in the sense that we can properly say only that there is mental ability "sort of stuff" which is responsible for these behaviors. Without further investigation, we are not able to say how many abilities are involved, what their specific natures are, how they are related, developed, etc. The relationship between observable behaviors and mental powers is in the first instance marked by ambiguity. The ambiguity is caused by the fact that there is not necessarily a one-to-one correspondence between observable behaviors and the mental powers which people have. It is possible for the same mental power to give rise to different observable behavior-types, and for different mental powers to result in the same observable behavior-types.

That is, according to the view of mental abilities being assumed here, there is no straightforward way to pass from the observation of people's behavior to the ascription of *specific* mental abilities to them. In the first place, the fact that a person does something does not mean that the person is able to do that thing. It is possible for a person to behave in a certain way without there being anything about his or her nature which is responsible for that behavior. The cause may, for example, reside outside the person in some external influence. On the other hand, the fact that a person behaves in a certain way, particularly if this behavior is of a type consistently observed in that person, provides on-the-face-of-it evidence that a mental ability of *some* sort is involved. Thus, the fact that a child consistently gets addition sums correct in arithmetic class indicates that the child has an ability to solve addition sums. But what the *specific* nature of this ability is, how it is related and differentiated from other abilities, and whether there is just one ability we would wish to call "ability to solve addition sums" remains unclear at this initial stage.

In order to provide specific detail on the meaning of the claim that the child has an ability to do addition sums, scientific research is needed. Specifically, research results which provide insight into the nature of the mental structures and mechanisms through which the child (and other people) solve addition sums are required. We need to know the mental processes which the child uses to solve the problems, and how these mental processes are related to reading processes, logical processes, aesthetic processes, etc., and how these processes arise from mental structures. Only then will we be able to say what we mean by "ability to solve addition sums." Do we mean that the person has some ability which is specific to solving addition sums and thus differentiable from other mathematical abilities? Do we mean that the child possesses some broader numerical competence which involves as a part the ability to solve addition problems? Do we mean that the child possesses a context-, mood-, belief- and attitude-independent mental ability, which enables the child to solve addition sums no matter what contextual influences may be operative, no matter what his or her mood or attitude, and no matter what empirical beliefs are held about the context in which the addition problems arise? We can only speculate about the answers to these questions until the relevant facts about the underlying nature of human mental abilities are known.

What now can be said about the definition of "critical thinking ability"? First of all, to the extent that Ennis wishes to remain at the level of providing a programmatic definition and of exhorting educators to adopt what he takes to be a valuable conception of the educated person, then his definitional strategy is a legitimate procedure to use.[9] However, McPeck's charge that Ennis has adopted a naive view of logical positivism has shifted the debate to a new plane. Logical positivism is a philosophy of scientific methodology, so McPeck seems concerned that Ennis is doing science poorly. To the extent that Ennis is involved in doing science, McPeck may be correct. At the present time there is no *scientific* legitimacy to grouping together a number of abilities and saying they go together to make up a larger ability. In addition, there is no scientific legitimacy to Ennis's claim that critical thinking ability involves ability to control for content and complexity, ability to interpret and apply, and ability to use sound principles of thinking.[10] If anything, the scientific evidence suggests that human mental abilities are content- and context-bound, and highly influenced by the complexity of the problems being addressed.[11]

Finally, it should be added that even if Ennis is involved solely in an exercise in programmatic definition, the way in which the scientific evidence turns out might influence how we would wish to portray that definition. For example, if control for contextual differences, one's empirical beliefs, and the content of problems are found to be related more to human attitude than to reasoning, then Ennis might wish to remove them from the umbrella of critical thinking. It might be more effective to develop attitudes in a separate manner.

The generalizability of critical thinking

The question of the generalizability of critical thinking flows quite naturally from broad definitions of the sort provided by Ennis. Many people advocate the promotion of critical thinking ability because they take it to be applicable to a wide variety, if not all areas, of human concern. Thus, the argument goes, if only the students graduating from our schools were good critical thinkers, then not only would they be able to use that ability in understanding the traditional disciplines, but also they would be able to apply the ability to solving problems and reaching decisions in situations encountered in the normal course of daily affairs.

John McPeck on the other hand claims that critical thinking is not a generalized ability. Critical thinking, he maintains, "can only be taught as part of a specific subject and never in isolation."[12] In part, McPeck takes this claim to be a conceptual truth. "Critical thinking is linked conceptually with particular activities and special fields of knowledge."[13] Despite this allegation of conceptual linkage between critical thinking and special fields of knowledge, the evaluation of which is grist for the philosopher's mill, there is an aspect of this issue which lies within the realm of science. The question of whether or not people can apply the *same* critical thinking ability to a number of fields is a question of whether or not the same mental power operates in different contexts. This is *not* a conceptual question, but a scientific one.

As it turns out, McPeck seems to recognize that there are empirical elements to the question of the generalizability of critical thinking ability. In particular, in the following argument for rejecting critical thinking as a generalizable ability, he appeals to many empirical claims:

> My reasons for rejecting the notion of reasoning . . . as a general skill are these: First, the term "reasoning" does not denote any particular process, performance or type of achievement, but rather a variety of them; second, the variety of things that we can and do reason about is so diverse that no one set of skills can produce competence in reasoning about all of them; third, we can, at best, teach people how to reason in specific areas and in connection with specific types of problem, but the various types of reasoning have too little in common to be considered a single skill.

I see the above three claims as the outline of a research agenda into an important and largely unexplored domain, rather than as an effective argument for rejecting the view that critical thinking is a generalized ability. That is, while McPeck offers them as assertions, the three would better have been stated as questions, the answers to which would provide some of the information required to decide on the generalizability of critical thinking. Thus transformed into questions, we can take a brief look at the research they would foster.

The first question would concern the denotation of *reasoning*, which would involve the same sorts of exploration used to determine the denotation of any natural kind of term. It would be necessary to carry out scientific investigations into the underlying nature of reasoning, possibly by constructing models of the component mental processes which comprise reasoning and by attempting to gather evidence to test the accuracy of these models. It is this sort of task which occupies information processing theorists and researchers, and this work would be highly relevant to the question of what the term *reasoning* denotes.

The second question which would arise from McPeck's claims is related closely to the issue of the referent of *reasoning,* but can be treated from another perspective. The question is whether there can be one set of reasoning skills which can produce competence in the large variety of areas in which human beings reason. McPeck's answer is that there cannot be. However, this judgment is premature. There are not *a priori* grounds for maintaining that there cannot be a single set of underlying reasoning processes which combine in intricate ways to produce the immense variety of reasoning which we witness at the behavioral level. We know already, for example, that three atomic particles and their very small number of properties can account for the existence, properties, and behaviors of over one hundred elementary substances. Surely, the possibility exists for the same to occur in the domain of human reasoning, but scientific investigation is required before sound pronouncements can be made on the extent of this possibility.

The third question would concern whether people can be taught to reason only within the contexts of specific types of problems. At present there exists quite a large body of evidence relevant to this question,[14] and much of it supports McPeck's contention that people cannot be taught thinking skills which they can apply across *different* contexts. However, the evidence relates primarily to the extent to which people can use deductive reasoning in different contexts. There exists a need to conduct similar research about critical thinking more broadly construed.

There is then a considerable amount of research to be done before claims such as McPeck's about the generalizability of critical thinking abilities can be substantiated. As I see it, this is not primarily philosophical work, but philosophers could contribute a good deal if they saw fit to do so. One of the prime areas which could profit from philosophical skills is the production of unambiguously testable claims about the generalizability of critical thinking ability. For example, is McPeck's claim that "we can at best teach people how to reason in connection with specific types of problems" testable? What sort of investigation would produce information relevant to its evaluation? If I teach students how to evaluate eyewitness testimony, and find that there is a concomitant increase in their ability to evaluate the observations made in science class, would this count as negative evidence? If I conduct a study and find that the majority of a large sample of adults are able to reason soundly about investing for their retirement without having had any instruction in this type of problem, would this count as negative evidence? These are questions about which philosophers can have important things to say. If philosophers do not wish to become involved in such questions, then I can only suggest that they either refrain from making unsupported empirical claims about critical thinking, or suffer the ridicule of those (like my reviewer) who see philosophy as irrelevant.

The validity of critical thinking tests

A mental ability test is valid when degree of the ability the test is designed to measure tends, among the group for which the test is designed, to be the cause of performance on the test. No test, just like no measuring instrument of any sort, can function properly in all possible circumstances. A test has to be designed to fit a niche defined by such things as the background knowledge of the people for whom the test is intended, the sorts of conditions which are to exist at the time of administering the test, and the type of interpretation which is to be put on test results. Whether or not a test fulfills its intended role is largely an empirical matter which can be examined.

In this section I wish to examine interpretations of two critical thinking tests. The first is Robert Ennis's interpretation that the keying of certain items on the *Watson-Glaser Critical Thinking Appraisal, Form A*[15] "depends upon value judgments about which there is possible disagreement and which are not constitutive of critical thinking."[16] The second is John McPeck's claim that the items on the induction section of the *Cornell Critical Thinking Test, Level Z*[17] "are currently questions of reading comprehension more than anything else."[18]

Ennis deals with a question from the Watson-Glaser test about whether a strong labor party would promote the general welfare of the people of the United States. Examinees are offered arguments for and against this position and are to judge whether those arguments are weak or strong. Ennis shows, correctly I believe, that one's political leanings could color one's interpretation of the strength of the arguments. What a Marxist judges to be a strong argument, a conservative might judge to be weak. Thus, people would be differentiated by the test because of their values (political persuasions) and not because of their level of critical thinking ability. If this occurs, the validity of the Watson-Glaser test would be diminished because people's value orientations and not their critical thinking ability would be the cause of their performance on those items. If . . . but what if things do not happen this way? What if the value orientations of the audience for whom this test is designed are sufficiently similar that differences in value play no significant role in determining differences in performance on the test? If this were the case, and it seems that Glaser believes it is,[19] then Ennis's objection would be no threat to the validity of the test, at least for its intended audience. The point I wish to make, of course, is that we do not know what is the case in this situation, and empirical work is needed to determine it. The philosophical role which Ennis played when pointing out the possible source of invalidity is valuable, but it will come to naught without complementary investigation into the soundness of his speculation.

McPeck's criticism of the Cornell test is based upon his perusal of the questions on the test and his perception that there was a large amount of material to read in comparison to the difficulty of the inferences examinees were asked to make. Thus, he concluded that the induction questions are questions of reading comprehension. Robert Ennis has already addressed this challenge to what his test "really tests" and, I believe, has provided a sound analysis. His view of "really-test-for" claims such as these is similar to my view of validity claims. To say what a test really tests is to ascribe performance on the test to a particular cause. Thus, Ennis contends, the evaluation of McPeck's charge awaits evidence from empirical research into the causes of performance on the Cornell test. The type of analysis which McPeck has provided, being based on inspection of questions on a test, is valuable as a source of hypotheses about threats to test validity. However, such hypotheses need to be tested empirically, and it has been my experience in designing and validating mental ability tests[20] that our intuitions about which factors will influence examinees' test performance are often far off the mark.

Concluding remarks

The thrust of this paper has been to argue that many of the questions about critical thinking which philosophers have historically treated involve empirical issues to a significant degree. I have urged that philosophers have not paid adequate heed to this fact, and that they should begin to do so. I have concentrated primarily on the work of Robert Ennis and John McPeck, but the issue pervades the field. Specifically, philosophers have said many relevant things about the definition of "critical thinking" and about the generalizability of critical thinking ability across different content areas. However, to the extent that these issues shade into empirical questions concerning the psychological nature of human mental abilities, then they should be treated as such, either by philosophers so inclined or by empirical researchers sensitive to the relevant philosophical issues. In addition, philosophers can contribute a great deal to the improvement of critical thinking tests, by working on the theory which supports the keying of answers on such tests, and by suggesting hypotheses about possibly invalidating factors. However, such hypotheses require empirical test. If there are philosophers inclined to run such tests, then they should proceed. Otherwise, they should forcefully indicate to empirical researchers the sorts of questions that require exploration.

CHAPTER 7

McPeck, informal logic, and the nature of critical thinking

Harvey Siegel

There is at present an unprecedented interest in critical thinking (henceforth CT). National commissions on the state of education decry the lack of emphasis on the development of reasoning ability in schools and call for the inclusion of reasoning in the curriculum as the fourth "R"; educators of all stripes belittle rote memorization in favor of educational programs which teach students how to think; entire university systems require their students to take courses in CT before graduation. It is a good time to be in the CT business.

Alongside the rise in interest in CT, recent years have witnessed the growth of the Informal Logic Movement (henceforth ILM). ILM arose largely as a response to the domination of logic by formal methods, and with the conviction that formal logic did little to enhance the reasoning ability of students, especially with regard to the sort of reasoning required in ordinary, everyday situations. Within the ILM it is widely held that logic, construed informally, has much to contribute to the educational task of enhancing students' reasoning ability. Consequently, many persons within ILM consider it to be a leading force in the general educational effort to enhance reasoning ability, and construe it as a focus both for the intellectual clarification of the nature of reasoning and argument, and for the practical, political, and pedagogical tasks of establishing critical thinking as an effective and central curricular effort.[1] In short, ILM and CT appear to be inextricably intertwined.

So there appears to be, at least in the minds of some, a close connection between CT, informal logic, and education. While some attention has been paid, in the literature of ILM, to the role of reasoning in education and to other aspects of CT, that literature has not, in my view, paid sufficient attention to questions concerning the nature of CT, the connec-

This paper is taken from part 1 of my "Educating Reason: Critical Thinking, Informal Logic, and the Philosophy of Education." Part 1, "A Critique of McPeck and a Sketch of an Alternative View," *American Philosophical Association Newsletter on Teaching Philosophy* 1985. Part 2, "Philosophical Questions Underlying Education for Critical Thinking," *Informal Logic 7* (1985). I am grateful to many for helpful comments on earlier versions of these papers, including Robin Barrow, Ralph Johnson, Stephen Norris, Bruce Suttle, Jeffrey Tlumak, and especially J. Anthony Blair and John McPeck. This work was supported in part by a grant from Michigan Technological University, for which I am also most grateful.

tion between informal logic and CT, or the larger questions of educational aims and ideals which a commitment to CT inevitably raises. ILM's commitment to CT is, I think, fraught with philosophical difficulties, difficulties which the movement neglects at its peril. In what follows I focus on one particular problem area ILM faces, for I believe the ILM, if it is to continue to construe itself as centrally concerned (either theoretically or pedagogically) with CT, must face much more squarely the important task of developing a satisfactory account of that notion. The remainder of this paper is an attempt to develop such an account.

John McPeck's recent work has also challenged ILM, and has similarly suggested that ILM endeavor to improve its problematic conception of CT. It is therefore appropriate to consider McPeck's analysis alongside the development of my own. This I do throughout the following discussion.

The nature of critical thinking

Much of the literature of ILM regards CT as a generalized skill or ability (or set of such skills and abilities). In his recent book *Critical Thinking and Education,*[2] however, John McPeck challenges this conception of CT. McPeck argues that CT cannot be properly regarded as a generalized skill, because there is no—and cannot be any—single critical thinking skill that can be applied generally across subject-area domains. This is because, according to McPeck, thinking (critical or otherwise) is never thinking *simpliciter,* it is always thinking about something or other: "Thinking is always thinking *about* something. To think about nothing is a conceptual impossibility."[3] On this basis, McPeck criticizes the sort of informal logic/CT course associated with ILM, namely, a course which seeks to enhance students' thinking ability *in general,* i.e., without regard to any particular subject matter:

> In isolation from a particular subject, the phrase "critical thinking" neither refers to nor denotes any particular skill. It follows from this that it makes no sense to talk about critical thinking as a distinct subject and that it therefore cannot profitably be taught as such. To the extent that critical thinking is not about a specific subject X, it is both conceptually and practically empty. The statement "I teach critical thinking," *simpliciter,* is vacuous because there is no generalized skill properly called critical thinking.[4]

There are some obvious difficulties with this argument. Most fundamentally, it confuses thinking generally (i.e., as denoting a *type* of activity) with specific *acts* (i.e., tokens) or instances of thinking. McPeck's claim that, "thinking . . . is logically connected to an X"[5] belies this confusion. A given act of thinking may, as McPeck suggests, always be about something or other; it may make no sense to say of a given episode of thinking that the thinker was thinking, but not about anything in particular. But it hardly follows from this that thinking, conceived as a general sort of activity which includes as instances all cases of particular acts of thinking about something—and such a conception must be possible, on pain of inability to identify all the specific acts as acts *of thinking*—must itself be construed as about something or other. It is not the case that the general activity of thinking is "logically connected to an X," any more than the general activity of cycling is logically connected to any particular bicycle. It is true that any given act of cycling must be done on some bicycle or other. But it surely does not follow that the general activity of cycling cannot be discussed independently of any particular bicycle. Indeed, we can state, and teach people, general skills of cycling (e.g., "Lean to the left when making a left-hand turn," "Slow down before cornering, not during cornering," etc.), even though instantiating these maneuvers and so exhibiting mastery of the general skills requires some particular bicycle.

As with cycling, so with thinking. Thus, McPeck's suggestion that teaching CT *simpliciter* is a conceptual impossibility is mistaken. As we can teach cycling, so we can teach CT. It makes perfect sense, for example, to claim that one teaches CT, *simpliciter,* when one means that one helps students to develop reasoning skills which are general in that they can be applied to many diverse situations and subject matters. *Contra* McPeck, there is nothing vacuous or unintelligible about such a claim. This point is supported, moreover, by the fact that there are readily identifiable reasoning skills which do not refer to any specific subject matter, which do apply to diverse situations, and which are in fact the sort of skill which courses in CT seek to develop. Skills such as identifying assumptions, tracing relationships between premises and conclusions, identifying standard fallacies, and so on, do not require the identification of specific subject matters: such skills are germane to thinking in subject areas as diverse as physics, religion, and photography. So McPeck's argument that CT is necessarily subject-specific and not generalizable, so that education efforts (e.g., courses) aimed at developing general critical thinking skills are conceptually confused, is not compelling. It fails to distinguish between specific acts of thinking and thinking conceived as a general type of activity (which allows the identification of those specific acts as acts *of thinking*), and it fails to take seriously obvious examples of general (i.e., not subject-specific) critical thinking skills and abilities.[6]

Having criticized the conception of CT as a (set of) generalized skill(s), McPeck offers a positive account of that notion. Noting that CT "involves a certain skepticism, or suspension of assent,"[7] and that such skepticism must be reflective and judicious, McPeck suggests the CT is "the appropriate use of *reflective skepticism* within the problem area under consideration."[8] Applying his earlier contention regarding the necessity of subject matter for CT, McPeck argues that CT is properly understood as subject-specific:

> Since critical thinking is always "critical thinking about X," it follows that critical thinking is intimately connected with other fields of knowledge. Thus the criteria for the judicious use of skepticism are supplied by the norms and standards of the field under consideration.[9]

After chiding informal logicians for neglecting or denying this "simple insight"[10] regarding the connection between CT and specific subjects or fields, and so for conceiving CT/informal logic as subject-neutral, Mc-Peck suggests that "the core meaning of critical thinking is the propensity and skill to engage in an activity with reflective skepticism."[11] McPeck emphasizes that this propensity and skill require thorough familiarity with the subject matter defining the activity; simply knowing some subject-neutral logic is not sufficient for CT: "There is no set of supervening skills that can replace basic knowledge of the field in question."[12] And McPeck offers the following "more formal" expression of the concept of CT:

> Let X stand for any problem or activity requiring some mental effort.
> Let E stand for the available evidence from the pertinent field or problem area.
> Let P stand for some proposition or action within X.
> Then we can say of a given student S that he is a critical thinker in the area X if S had the disposition and skill to do X in such a way that E, or some subset of E, is suspended as being sufficient to establish the truth or viability of P.[13]

Notice first that the notion of "reflective skepticism" is opaque. A skeptic might be reflective, and yet her skepticism unjustified. And it will not do to justify skepticism in terms of its appropriateness, such appropriateness being determined by disciplinary or problem-area criteria, for often it is just those criteria which one needs to be reflectively skeptical about.

The act of suspension McPeck highlights in his "formal" expression of the concept of CT is worth a bit more scrutiny. Here I think McPeck is importantly right about something, although his concern with grinding his "subject-specific" axe has obscured the important point he makes. Appreciating this point clearly, moreover, leads the way to an incisive reformulation of the concept of CT.

What is it for a critical thinker to have "the disposition and skill to do X in such a way that E (the available evidence from a field) is suspended (or temporarily rejected) as sufficient to establish the truth or viability of P (some proposition or action within X)?"[14] It is simply to say that the critical thinker has the disposition and skill to question the power of E to warrant P. That is, the critical thinker has the disposition and skill to ask whether E actually provides compelling reasons for P, or justifies P. This is, I think, the defining characteristic of CT: the focus on reasons and the power of reasons to warrant or justify beliefs, claims, and actions. A critical thinker, then, is one who is *appropriately moved by reasons:* she has a propensity or disposition to believe and act in accordance with reasons, and she has the ability to assess the force of reasons in the many contexts in which reasons play a role. McPeck rightly notes the two central components of this conception of CT. There is, first, the ability to properly assess reasons. Call this the *reason assessment* component. There is, second, the willingness, desire, and disposition to base one's actions and beliefs on reasons, that is, to *do* reason assessment and to be guided by the results of such assessment. This I call the *critical attitude* or *critical spirit* component of CT. Both components are, I claim, essential to the proper conception of CT, the possession of which are necessary for the achievement of CT by a person. They are jointly sufficient as well. The concept of CT is captured by this "appropriately moved by reasons" (henceforth AMR) conception.[15]

Although McPeck's conception of CT hinges on the notion of "reflective skepticism," which I have argued is defective in certain ways, it is important to note that McPeck's analysis does recognize the components of, and is largely compatible with, the AMR conception. As has already been pointed out, McPeck's formal expression explicitly mentions the critical spirit component of the concept of CT, and his subsequent discussion emphasizes this component: "It is sufficient for our purposes to recognize that training in particular critical thinking skills is not sufficient to produce a critical thinker. One must also develop the disposition to use those skills."[16] McPeck also emphasizes the central role of the reason assessment component in CT. He labels his approach to CT "epistemological" rather than "logical," because it focuses on the epistemology of various subject areas rather than on subject-neutral logic, and he notes that "the epistemological approach to critical thinking involves little more than providing . . . [an] understanding [of] what constitutes good reasons for various beliefs."[17]

McPeck's detailed articulation of his conception of CT thus approximates the AMR conception. However, his discussion often obscures this, for that discussion emphasizes issues which are tangential to the nature of CT, and in which McPeck takes positions which are problematic positions on those issues, thereby obscuring his correct identification of the two central components of the AMR conception of CT. I wish now to (a) consider three such tangential issues, (b) show how McPeck's discussion of them is problematic, and (c) argue that the AMR conception is independent of these issues, and stands untouched by criticisms of McPeck's discussion of them.

McPeck is emphatic in his insistence that logic (formal or informal) is either largely or entirely irrelevant to CT. He writes that:

> the real problem with uncritical students is not a deficiency in a general skill, such as logical ability, but rather a more general lack of education in the traditional sense . . . I shall attempt to show why courses in logic fail to accomplish the goal of developing critical thinkers and how the epistemology of various subjects would be the most reasonable route to that end . . . There is both a conceptual and a pedagogic link between epistemology, critical thinking, and education, but the study of logic or critical thinking as such has no part in this linkage.[18]

> The standard approach for developing critical thinking . . . has been to teach logic and various kinds of general reasoning skills. Presumably, the rationale for this approach is that since logic plays a role in every subject, and logic is intimately related to reasoning, the study of logic should improve one's ability to assess arguments and statements in any subject area. What I wish to argue is that the plausibility of this reasoning can be sustained only by seriously underestimating the complexity of the different kinds of information used in arguments and by overestimating the role of logic in these assessments. That is, even when the problem at issue is the rational assessment of some statement or argument, the major requirements for such assessment are epistemological, not logical, in character.[19]

I note in passing McPeck's ambivalence as to whether logic is *entirely* irrelevant to CT, or only *largely* irrelevant (so that logic is at least somewhat relevant). The former citation makes the first, stronger claim; the latter makes only the second, weaker claim.

As noted earlier, McPeck agrees that reason assessment is a central component of CT—indeed, he emphasizes the point, since his "epistemological approach" places reason assessment at the heart of CT. Thus, logic can be irrelevant to CT for McPeck only if logic has nothing to do with reason assessment. But this is false on its face: even if many, or even most, reasons are properly assessed only with reference to subject-specific criteria, some (and perhaps many or most) reasons are properly assessed at least partially in accordance with subject-neutral logical reasons. The fallacies furnish obvious examples here. To take just one: when Jehovah's Witnesses come to my door, and argue that I should believe in the divinity of the Bible because (for the reason that) the Bible proclaims itself to be the divine word of God, it does not take any theological or other subject-specific information or criteria to realize that the reason offered does not in fact support the claim it is offered in support of. Rather, it begs the question. Here logic is relevant to reason assessment, and so is relevant to CT, even on McPeck's own terms. This example illustrates the relevance of *informal* logic to reason assessment, and so to CT as McPeck construes it.

Similarly, *formal* logic is relevant to CT. First, formal logic can be seen as providing a paradigm of good argumentation. A deductively valid formal argument is as strong an argument as it is possible to have; the connection between the premises and conclusion of such an argument is as tight as any such connection can be. To put the point slightly differently: formal argumentation may profitably be seen as constituting an "ideal type" of argument, which (like ideal types in social science, or "ideal laws" like the ideal gas laws in physical science) may not be typically, or ever, encountered in everyday discourse, but which nevertheless are central to our theoretical understanding of argumentation. Thus, formal logic is a crucial component of an adequate conception of CT.

A second reason for thinking formal logic to be relevant to CT is that the latter is fundamentally concerned with the proper assessment of reasons, and formal logic provides an excellent source of clear reasons. For example, it is hard to imagine a more compelling reason for accepting some proposition Q than the proposition "PvQ.-P" ("P or Q, and not P"). Given the latter proposition, we have conclusive reason for accepting the former. In fact, propositions which deductively entail some other proposition seem to me to be the most compelling reasons there can be for accepting the latter proposition. Thus, formal logic is relevant to reason assessment, and so to CT (and exposure to formal logic is desirable for the CT student, for it illustrates well the fundamental property of "being a reason for").[20]

Thus, logic (both formal and informal) is relevant to reason assessment, and so to CT, on McPeck's terms as well as my own. Logic is relevant to the determination of the goodness of reasons. Such determination is central to CT. Thus, his claim that logic is irrelevant (either largely or totally) to CT is mistaken.

The relation of logic to information

McPeck draws a sharp distinction not only between logic and CT. He also[21] distinguishes sharply between logic and (nonlogical, subject-specific) information, and argues that the assessment of good reasons is determined (largely or wholly) by the latter. We have already seen that McPeck claims that "the major requirements for [the rational assessment of statements or arguments] are epistemological, not logical in character."[22] His view is that the assessment of good reasons is dependent, not on logic, but on specialized, field-dependent knowledge:

> Typically we are in a quandary less about the logical validity of an argument than about the truth of the putative evidence. We frequently cannot determine whether evidence is good or not, because such a judgement depends upon special knowledge. One has to be a fellow participant in the particular domain of meaning to appreciate the proper significance of the evidence.[23]

> Critical thinking is linked conceptually with particular activities and special fields of knowledge.[24]

> Specific content, knowledge and information cannot be coherently demarcated from critical thinking.[25]

McPeck is at least right here: the assessment of reasons often involves essential appeal to information which is subject-specific or field-dependent. But there are difficulties here as well. First, McPeck shifts, as earlier, between stronger and weaker claims: that logic is entirely irrelevant to reason assessment, or that it is only somewhat irrelevant (and so somewhat relevant) to such assessment; that information is sufficient for reason assessment, or only necessary for such assessment; that information is always necessary for reason assessment or only sometimes necessary. McPeck writes, for example, that:

> a minimal condition for understanding a good reason in any field is that one understands the full meaning of the specialized and often technical language in which such reasons are expressed.[26]

True enough, in cases in which reasons are expressed in specialized and technical language. But frequently reasons are expressed in nonspecialized, nontechnical language. In such cases full understanding does not require mastery of specialized language. Reasoning occurs in specialized and technical, but also in nonspecialized and nontechnical, areas. Thus McPeck's weaker claim that specialized information is sometimes required for reason assessment is sustained, but the stronger claim that it is always required is not. (How typical each sort of case is is an empirical matter.) Moreover, the weaker claim is an important point for critical thinkers to appreciate, but it is not itself a subject-specific point; it is rather a general point about reason assessment that could well be made in a general critical thinking course. Thus, McPeck's weaker claim is well taken. But it must not be confused with the stronger claim. Nor does it cast any general doubt on the utility of a general course in CT. Indeed, points like the ones McPeck is concerned to make—e.g. that specialized knowledge is often required for reason assessment— themselves belong to no specific field; to the extent that they are important points for critical thinkers to grasp, it seems highly appropriate to present them in a domain-neutral CT course. Thus, McPeck's argument does not only undermine, it actually suggests the practical necessity or utility of, general CT courses: such courses are important if there is general information—like McPeck's point, and like logic—that it is important for students to have.

If there is a viable distinction to be drawn between logic and information, they are both relevant to reason assessment and so to CT. McPeck does well to remind us of the importance of general information, or the inappropriateness of general CT courses.

The relation of CT to rationality

We have already seen McPeck's emphasis on the role of good reasons in CT. This naturally raises the question of the relation of CT to rationality. McPeck suggests that CT is a subspecies of rationality, but that the latter far outstrips the former:

> While critical thinking is perfectly compatible with rationality, and with reasoning generally, we should not regard the terms as equivalent. The concept of critical thinking denotes a particular type of thinking . . . No injustice to rationality will result from simply construing it as the *intelligent use of all available evidence* for the solution of some problem. There are, of course, difficulties with the notion of evidence (what, for example, is to count as evidence?). Also, rationality may sometimes countenance the disregarding of certain types of evidence. But it is precisely from these problematic junctures in reasoning that critical thinking derives its conceptual content and it is here the employment of critical thinking is perhaps most useful. Indeed, it requires critical thinking even to recognize that one has arrived at such a juncture. All of this does not make critical thinking distinct from, much less incompatible with, rationality; rather rationality includes critical thinking as a particular aspect (or subset) of itself. The concept of critical thinking merely marks out the facet of rationality that comprises the disposition and skill to find such difficulties in the normal course of reasoning.[27]

McPeck seems to suggest here that rationality is broader than CT in that, while rationality includes within its domain all instances of the intelligent use of evidence in the solution of problems, CT involves only some of those instances: namely those instances in which the determination of relevant evidence is problematic. When one is engaged in intelligent problem solving, one is within the domain of rationality; when one is engaged in such a way that it is necessary to raise "meta-questions" about the constitution, relevance, or appropriateness of putative pieces of evidence to the solution of the problem at hand, one is in the subdomain of CT within the larger domain of rationality. CT is a particular sort of rational thinking which takes place in a particular sort of problem-solving context.

The distinction McPeck draws here between CT and rationality is untenable. McPeck limits the range of CT to cases in which reasons or evidence are in some ways problematic, and to reasoning about the problematic nature of reasons or evidence in question. But this restriction is not argued for. It is, moreover, incompatible with McPeck's earlier articulation of his "epistemological approach" to CT, according to which CT involves the skill and disposition to seek out, understand, and base belief and action upon good reasons. If McPeck is to maintain his "epistemological" or "good reasons" approach to CT, then he must reject the limitation he seems to want to place on the range of CT in his distinction between CT and rationality. The reason assessment component of CT extends to the assessment of all reasons, not just "meta-reasons" concerning the constitution, relevance or appropriateness of problematic "ground floor" reasons.

Once one rejects this limitation on the range of CT, the distinction between CT and rationality collapses. CT is coextensive with rationality, not merely a dimension for it, for rationality is "coextensive with the relevance of reasons,"[28] as is CT. The connection between rationality and reasons is as tight as can be. As Larry Laudan puts it:

> At its core, rationality . . . consists in doing (or believing) things because we have good reasons for doing so . . . If we are going to determine whether a given action or belief is (or was) rational, we must ask whether there are (or were) sound reasons for it.[29]

Insofar as rationality consists of believing and acting on the basis of good reasons, and insofar as we accept McPeck's epistemological approach to CT (or an approach which makes reason assessment central), we must perforce regard CT not as a dimension of rationality, but as its equivalent or educational cognate. Thus, the distinction McPeck draws between CT and rationality cannot be sustained.

It is time to regain the thread of the overall argument. I have been arguing that McPeck's discussions of the relations between logic and CT, logic and information, and CT and rationality are in their various ways problematic. This should not obscure the fact that we are fundamentally agreed that CT centrally involves reason assessment and the disposition to engage in it, that is, that CT involves both the reason assessment component and the critical spirit component of the AMR conception. That conception is unbesmirched by the difficulties with McPeck's analysis which I have been belaboring for the last few pages. In the end McPeck is importantly right about the nature of CT, despite those difficulties.

Conclusion

If the AMR conception of CT is correct, two large sets of philosophical issues are of crucial importance for the analysis and theory of CT, and so for ILM. The first involves the relationship between CT and the philosophy of education; the second, the relationship between CT and epistemology. The first of these sets of issues, concerning the relationship between ILM, CT, and the philosophy of education, the justification of CT as an educational ideal, and the justification of educational interventions aimed at the fostering of CT skills and dispositions in students, is particularly germane for this audience. I regret that space forbids pursuit of these important and exciting issues.[30]

I hope, however, that our time here has not been wasted. For central to these issues is the notion of CT, a notion which is far from clear. Important theoretical and practical work hinges on it. To the extent that light has been shed on it, work in informal logic, educational psychology, educational policy, curriculum development, and pedagogy all stand to benefit.

McPeck's book has been fundamental to the clarification project. While not without its difficulties, *Critical Thinking and Education* has shaken ILM from its complacency with respect to the notion of critical thinking, and also with respect to its obliviousness to central issues in the philosophy of education. For philosophy of education, it has breathed new life into classical questions concerning, among others, educational aims and their justification, the role of logic in education, and the relationship between subject-specific information and "domain-neutral" information and their respective roles in the curriculum. Such breaths of fresh air do not come our way very often. We are all in McPeck's debt for sending this happy and refreshing gust our way.

CHAPTER 8

Response to Stephen Norris and Harvey Siegel on the analysis of *Critical Thinking and Education*

John E. McPeck

I would first like to thank Stephen Norris and Harvey Siegel for their efforts and for providing such thoughtful and painstaking critiques of my general views about critical thinking. I, of course, am the major beneficiary of their efforts, as they have caused me to rethink certain things and to see dimensions of the problems associated with CT which might otherwise have escaped my attention.

Economy of effort would suggest that I treat both of their papers at once, but the different points made by each are so different that this is not feasible. Indeed, aside from their both finding fault with my views, the two critiques have so little in common that I doubt that Norris and Siegel themselves could find much to agree about with respect to where I have gone wrong. I doubt, for example, that Siegel would find much merit in seeking underlying psychological causes of CT abilities, as Norris does. I believe Siegel, like myself, would find the question of *causes* of abilities to be largely a red herring in this context. But I'm not sure of Siegel's view here. In any case, let me turn to Norris's paper first.

Norris's critique

You will recall that Norris begins his paper by observing that the so-called two cultures phenomenon exists between philosophers of education and scientists, who, ostensibly, never pay attention to one another. Indeed, Norris's paper is largely a plea for empiricism in matters having to do with "thinking abilities," and also an admonition to philosophers for making "pronouncements" which have empirical implications, although philosophers "never get their hands dirty actually doing science." I'm not sure just how true this is, because what it means to "do science" is a fairly broad and eclectic notion. I would think that anyone who pays due regard to empirical facts, and keeps abreast of the relevant empirical literature, could be said to be "doing science" in some defensible sense. One need not wear a white jacket and spend his time in a lab to be "doing science." Indeed, the Philosophy of Education Society has several members who focus their attention on, and spend the bulk of their time, analyzing various types of empirical claims and theories within psychology, sociology, and education generally. I'm thinking, for example, of D. C. Phillips, G. Fenstermacher, C. J. B. Macmillan, and several others, whose work on empirical claims could be considered "doing science" in this broader sense. To a lesser extent, I consider myself to be doing the same. But no doubt there is still merit in Norris's general admonition: an empirical perspective very often throws a different light on things. However, in this particular case, Norris's zeal to have us look at critical thinking more empirically results in his repeatedly confusing philosophical questions with empirical ones. The effect is to return to the darkness where there had been, at least, some light.

In what follows, I will present three lines of argument which support my charge that Norris seriously confuses philosophical questions with empirical ones, and that his particular plea for empiricism represents a retrograde step insofar as it represents both confused philosophy and gratuitous empiricism.

The first argument will attempt to show that Norris confuses *causal* questions, which are empirical, with questions of *meaning,* which are not. And that he does this in many places throughout his paper. The second argument will directly address what Norris considers to be the broad contention of his paper, namely, that I unwittingly make empirical pronouncements without recognizing them. I will argue, to the contrary, that most of Norris's claims about things being "empirical questions" are largely gratuitous, often question-begging, and generally at odds with good scientific practice. Finally, I'll discuss, rather briefly, the three specific assertions that Norris considers to be empirical questions which he regards as ripe for research.

Since this is a rather full agenda, let me begin straightaway with Norris's confusion of causes with meanings. The confusion first appears in Norris's general claim that we cannot really know what is meant by ascribing an ability to someone unless we understand what underlying mechanisms give rise to it. He says:

> In order to disambiguate the claim that the child has an ability to do addition sums, scientific research is needed. Specifically, research results which provide insight into the nature of the mental structures and mechanisms through which the child (and other people) solve addition sums are required. We need to know the mental processes which the child uses to solve the problems . . . Only then will we be able to say what we mean by "ability to solve addition sums."

I think this view is not only false, but would lead to a methodological absurdity if any scientist took it seriously. First, it is simply not true that we do not know what we mean when we ascribe an ability to someone if we are ignorant of the mental structures (or processes) which give rise to it. On the contrary, in almost every case where we ascribe abilities to someone (which is virtually all the time), we have no idea about any underlying structures. We often say, clearly and meaningfully, things like "Fisher has the ability to play chess," "Dr. J. has scoring ability," or "Jones has writing ability," when we do not have the slightest idea about what mental structures (or mechanisms) are at work when people perform those tasks. Indeed, neither scientists nor anyone else can claim to understand the precise mental structures which underlie any human ability, yet this brute fact does not stop us from making ability judgments one whit. We all understand, for example, what is meant when someone says, "Jones can speak French," even though we do not know what underlying structures might account for this ability. This is because in ascribing abilities to someone we are not talking about *causes* of abilities, but about the capacity to *perform*. Much less are we talking about the physiological "hard-wiring" or reductionistic types of causes which Norris seems to have in mind.

We might notice in this connection that it is never clear in Norris's paper which level of causality he believes necessary to understand before we can ascribe abilities. Sometimes he claims a knowledge of "mental structures" is necessary, and at other times he talks about "mechanisms," and provides analogies with "magnetism" and atomic structures of molecules. It seems to me that if Norris wants to claim that scientific knowledge is necessary for the ascription of abilities, then it is incumbent upon him to specify at which level it is necessary to have knowledge, and why it is specifically *that* level and not some other. He never addresses this question, but merely says "empirical knowledge" is necessary. (This, incidentally, is one of the reasons I regard his call for empiricism as largely gratuitous.)

Norris's preoccupation with fundamental, bottom-up causes of abilities is further evidenced in this statement:

> Mental powers, in turn, arise from mental structures and processes in the same way that physical objects (magnetism is an example) arise from the internal structure and processes of physical objects.

The kinds of causal connections which Norris apparently has in mind here might be of some interest to people trying to model artificial intelligence, or to brain physiologists, but none of this has any bearing on the *meaning* of ability concepts, nor on our ability to ascribe them to people. To think that there is a direct bearing here, as Norris does, is to confuse the *cause of X* with the *meaning of X;* which, in turn, is to confuse the scientific question with the philosophical one.

Consider, further, the methodological absurdity that would be involved in a scientist seeking underlying causes of a certain ability if the scientist did not have some *antecedent* notion of what the ability was. Even scientists work with some *a priori* conceptions of the phenomena they choose to investigate. And very often philosophical analysis can provide extremely useful clarifications of these initial conceptions. But whether this is the good scientist doing some good philosophy, or *vice versa,* scientific and philosophical questions should not be confused with each other, because different *kinds* of evidence apply in each case.

Norris's confusion of causes with meaning can also be found in the following somewhat puzzling statement:

> In the first place, the fact that a person does something does not mean that a person *can* do that thing. It is possible for a person to behave in a certain way without there being anything about his or her nature which is responsible for that behavior. The cause may, for example, reside outside the person in some external influence.

Norris does not provide an example here; but I, for one, cannot envisage a case where a person does in fact *do* something, where we cannot say that the person *can do* that thing. Notice that Norris does not say that the person merely *appears* to do something, but that the person *does* it. Surely, if a person *does* something even at gunpoint, that is sufficient evidence that they *can* do it. Actually to *do,* logically implies *can.* The "cause" of a person's doing something is quite beside the point of the *ability* to do it. Again, Norris confuses *causal* questions with questions of *meaning.*

The second general criticism I have to make about Norris's paper is of his overall thesis that I am unknowingly engaged in making empirical "pronouncements," and that his paper is intended to show us how and where this occurs. As I have already mentioned, I believe this general thesis to be largely gratuitous, question-begging, and inconsistent with sound scientific practice. It is gratuitous because any conceptual analysis worth its salt will yield some empirical implications or consequences. Indeed, we usually hope that it does, else it is hardly worth doing in the first place. But this fact does not make the analysis itself empirical. Various philosophical analyses of things like "justice" or "duty" might be rife with serious empirical social consequences, but this does not render those analyses empirical. In the present case, I have offered an analysis of the concept "critical thinking," and I would hope that it may have some empirical consequences, but my analysis itself is not an empirical one.

Furthermore, Norris's general plea for empiricism is gratuitous in this connection because he seems simply to want to raise an entirely different set of questions about critical thinking from those that I have addressed. Norris wants to address questions about underlying "structures" and "mechanisms," and that is fine, if he so wishes. But neither I nor Ennis were talking about "structures" or "mechanisms"; we were talking about meanings, definitions, and pedagogical strategies. I do not see why Ennis or I should be faulted simply for not talking about the sorts of things that Norris is interested in. What is required of Norris's thesis is to show how his interest in underlying causes actually undermines or invalidates something that we have said. But he has not shown this. Nor has he explained why his causal questions about structures and mechanisms make any significant difference to how we teach or talk about different mental abilities. All that Norris has said, really, is that our analyses *may have* some interesting and different empirical implications. And this is where it sits. Thus, I view this general call for empiricism as gratuitous.

In addition, Norris's defense of the proposition that certain "mental powers" can give rise to different mental abilities, begs the very question to which I have been trying to draw attention. You will recall, for example, that I have argued against the coherence of the notion of a "generalized reasoning ability" (save for "general intelligence," or IQ perhaps) on the grounds that what we *mean* by, say, "mathematical reasoning" is logically distinct from "historical reasoning" or "moral reasoning." In brief, my rejection of the notion of "general reasoning ability" is similar to the reasons one might have for rejecting the general notion of, say, "ability to win at games." When one considers how many different games there are, from crosswords to chess, or from football to cricket, we soon realize that there is no singular "ability to win at games." Rather, we see that there are almost as many kinds of skills involved as there are different kinds of games. Similarly, I have argued, it makes more sense to conceive of "reasoning abilities" to be of logically different kinds, just as abilities to win at different kinds of games are different. And I have argued this case on conceptual grounds—i.e., what it *means* to do "mathematical reasoning" is logically distinct from what it *means* to do "moral reasoning."

Now whether or not one agrees with my rejection of "general reasoning ability" is not the point here. The point is that to simply posit the existence of general reasoning skills, or general "mental powers," as Norris calls them, is to beg the very question which I have challenged. That Norris does assume the existence of general reasoning skills can be seen from the fact that it is clearly embedded in most of his discussion. For example:

> Ability claims . . . are in my estimation categorical claims about people's either genetically or environmentally determined natures. Specifically, to say that someone has critical thinking ability is to make a claim about a mental power which that person possesses.

And elsewhere:

> It is possible for the same mental power to give rise to different observable behavior-types, and for different mental powers to result in the same observable behavior-type.

Whatever else Norris might mean by this mysterious phrase "mental powers," it is at least clear that it is to refer to some generalized power— much like a "general reasoning ability." But this is precisely the kind of general notion which I have been at pains to analyze and unpack as containing a plethora of conceptual muddles. Thus, it begs the question about the existence of "general abilities" in general, and "critical thinking" in particular.

And finally, Norris's introduction of the notion of "mental powers" is a retrograde step both from a philosophical and from a social scientific point of view. What, for example, does the phrase "mental powers" refer to specifically? Are we to regard "mental powers" as having some kind of ontological reality (e.g., the ghost in Descartes' machine?), or are they to be viewed as *theoretical constructs* like, say, "general intelligence"? This is not clear in Norris's discussion. But even if we liberally interpret the phrase as a theoretical construct, it blurs many useful distinctions about abilities which are otherwise clear. For example, even if we should discover that two different abilities (call them "A" and "B") should correlate highly with some other ability (call this "C"), this would still not render A and B the same ability. For example, if "achievement" and "social class" should both correlate substantially with IQ (which they do, incidentally!), this would not mean that "social class" and "achievement" are the same thing. I believe this is what the introduction of the phrase "mental powers" does.

Space does not permit development of the point here, but I believe in fact that what Norris may unwittingly mean by "mental power" is, at bottom, synonymous to what is normally meant by "general intelligence" (or IQ). Witness, again, his statement that

> ability claims . . . are in my estimation categorical claims about people's either genetically or environmentally determined natures. Specifically, to say that someone has critical thinking ability is to make a claim about a mental power which that person possesses.

If this isn't simply another way of describing "general intelligence" (or IQ), I don't know what is. And this kind of general notion—e.g., "mental power," intelligence, or Spearman's *g*—does not advance our knowledge or understanding of specific mental abilities, which is what we are all trying to understand and to teach. In this sense it is a retrograde step, which is largely beside the question at issue.

The third, and final, argument I wish to make is that Norris's proposed research agenda for investigating my three assertions about general reasoning skills will not produce the results he anticipates.

Towards the end of Norris's paper, you will recall, he quotes three of my reasons for rejecting the notion of reasoning as a generalized skill. He then attempts to show how each of these reasons are actually empirical questions (in his view), worthy of independent empirical investigation, and that such research might result in making a case for considering "reasoning" to be a "generalized ability."

The first reason I gave for not construing "reasoning" as a generalized ability was (and he quotes me): "The term 'reasoning' does not denote any particular process, performance or type of achievement, but rather a variety of them." Norris insists that this is an empirical assertion that requires scientific investigation which

> would concern the denotation of "reasoning," which would involve the same sorts of exploration used to determine the denotation of any natural kind term. It would be necessary to carry out scientific investigation into the underlying nature of reasoning . . . It is this sort of task which occupies information processing theorists and researchers, and this work would be highly relevant to the question of what the term "reasoning" denotes.

Three brief comments about this argument. First, the denotation, *qua* denotation, of common terms like "reasoning" is a *conceptual* question *par excellence,* and has nothing whatever to do with scientific investigation. (This is a dramatic example, again, of Norris simply confusing philosophical questions with scientific ones.) Second, talk of "natural kinds," and the scientific investigation of "natural kinds," in the way Norris uses this phrase, went out with Aristotelian science. What is a "natural kind"? And third, whatever empirical findings information processing theorists should discover, it would still not change the *denotation* of "reasoning" one whit. If they should discover, for example, that "walking" and "talking" had the same underlying structure (of some kind), this would still not change the denotation, as such, of "walking" and "talking."

The second reason I gave for not construing "reasoning" to be a generalized skill was (and he quotes me again): "The variety of things that we can and do reason about is so diverse that no one set of skills can produce competence in reasoning about all of them." To this, Norris responds that my "judgment is premature." He says:

> There are no *a priori* grounds for maintaining that there cannot be a single set of underlying reasoning processes which combine in intricate ways to produce the immense variety of reasoning which we witness at the behavioral level. We know already, for example, that three atomic particles and their very small number of properties can account for the existence, properties, and behaviors of over one hundred elementary substances.

Here we see Norris's preoccupation with reductionistic *causes* very much in evidence. Indeed, it looks like he might be talking about some kind of cortical "hard-wiring" to explain reasoning. In any case, I have several objections to this line of argument.

First, I am not talking about "underlying causes" of reasoning at some structural level, but about the different overt manifestations at the behavioral level. And at this publicly observable level there *are* some valid *a priori* grounds for saying, as I do, that there is not just *one* reasoning skill involved in the different kinds of reasoning tasks, but *several*. These *a priori* grounds are, very simply, that what would count as effective mathematical reasoning is different in kind from what counts as effective moral reasoning—i.e., "effective reasoning" means two different things in these instances, just as what counts as "playing effective soccer" is different from what counts as "playing effective checkers." Thus, there are some valid *a priori* grounds for considering the term "reasoning" to refer to many different skills, and not just one generic skill.

Second, we might notice that there is one almost tautological sense in which *all* reasoning skills are, in some trivial sense, connected to every other one. For example, they might all issue from one agent, or brain. But this is merely to say something like all types of reasoning require the agent to be *conscious;* or like saying the computer must be plugged in before it can perform its diverse tasks. Indeed, the computer metaphor is useful here. Norris, in effect, is talking about "hardware," like a new computer just lifted from the box with no software in it yet; whereas I am talking about "reasoning" as different kinds of software packets which must be written into the machine. Different individual programs must be written into the machine before it can produce its diverse performances. Now it is true, as Norris's view would suggest, that many different programs can run on the same wiring. But this fact still does not permit us to say that two different programs are in fact one, simply because they might employ the same wiring. Nor does this fact bypass the need to individually "input" different programs in order to get different kinds of performances. Thus, for both conceptual and pedagogical reasons, I think we are much further ahead by considering the different reasoning skills to be like different kinds of computer programs, requiring different "inputs" and "outputs," despite common wiring schemes. If it should turn out that moral reasoning should some-how employ certain common "underlying structures" with mathematical reasoning, we would still have every reason for considering them two different skills, and for treating them pedagogically as such (as we would in programming).

The third, and final, reason I gave for considering the term "reasoning" to refer to many distinct skills, and not just one, was that

we can, at best, teach people how to reason in specific areas and in connection with specific types of problems, but the various types of reasoning have too little in common to be considered a single skill. (McPeck)

This claim is, alas, an empirical claim, as Norris points out. (One out of three is not too bad, I guess!) However, I do not see in this claim any cause for jubilation about the prospects of teaching "general reasoning skills." I say this, not only for the sorts of reasons that I have just provided, but also because the available empirical evidence would appear to support my position, and not Norris's. Clearly, I cannot review the empirical literature here. However, Robert Glaser (University of Pittsburgh) does review this literature extensively in a lead article in the *American Psychologist* (February 1984) entitled "Education and Thinking: The Role of Knowledge." His conclusion is that the most responsible work being done in the fields of cognitive science, artificial intelligence research, and educational psychology are all clearly pointing in the direction that domain-specific knowledge is the main determinant of what we call "reasoning" and "reasoning skills." Thus, Norris is holding out for a kind of rear-guard hope for "generalized reasoning skill," which is not borne out by the available empirical evidence. Therefore, there remains little reason for changing our general pedagogical strategy of teaching people to think within the different knowledge domains; which, I submit, is what common sense had suggested to us in the first place.

Siegel's critique

You may have noticed that Siegel begins and ends his paper with some very kind remarks about my general approach to critical thinking (CT). I would, therefore, like your and my response to consist in simply remembering these favorable bits, and forgetting all the rest.

The truth is, there is much in Siegel's paper that I agree with, and about which I could (and perhaps should) make some equally kind remarks. However, being the strange animals that we philosophers are, I don't think that Siegel would be satisfied with this. So, in order to indulge that sadomasochistic streak in our enterprise which is criticism, I will instead restrict my comments to a few points in Siegel's paper which might provide some interesting (if not pleasurable) pain.

I will address my comments to Siegel's separate arguments in the order of their appearance. Unfortunately, his very first argument happens to be favorable towards me, so I shall skip this one— given our proclivities. His second argument, however, proves to be more arousing.

This second argument, you will recall, has to do with my rejection of general courses which are designed to teach CT *simpliciter*. I argued, among other things, that such courses really make very little sense, because *thinking,* as such, is always about some specific subject or thing (let's call this X). And to the extent that critical thinking is not about a specific subject X, it is both conceptually and practically empty. Thus, statements like "I teach critical thinking *simpliciter*" are vacuous because there is, upon analysis, no generalized skill properly called "critical thinking." On my view, there are almost as many skills involved in "critical thinking" as there are logically distinct kinds of things to think critically about. Critical thinking, like "reasoning," manifests itself in far more ways than any course in CT could hope to cover.

Siegel offers two related arguments against this point of view. The first is that

> it confuses thinking generally (i.e., as denoting a *type* of activity) with specific *acts* (i.e., tokens) or instances of thinking . . . A given act of thinking may, as McPeck suggests, always be about something or other; it may make no sense to say of a given episode of thinking that the thinker was thinking, but not about anything in particular. But it hardly follows from this that thinking, conceived as a general sort of activity which includes as instances all cases of particular acts of thinking about something . . . must itself be construed as about something or other.

While it's not too clearly put, there is a point in this argument which I am forced to acknowledge. It's a point which I had not recognized before, namely, that the phenomenon of thinking can itself be the object of our thinking, and it makes grammatical sense to say so. I accept this point. However, I do not think the argument accomplishes what it set out to do, namely, to undermine the two points which I had made about thinking. My first point was a *conceptual* one, namely, that "thinking" always requires some specific object X. To appreciate this point, notice that it is always appropriate to ask someone (within the bounds of good manners, of course) *what* they are thinking *about*. If they should truthfully report "nothing," then we would say that they were not really thinking. To think logically entails something to be thought *about*. And this general point remains true even if the object of our thinking should be thinking itself. Thus, the conceptual point stands.

My second point, on the other hand, was primarily a pedagogical one. I argued that thinking, specifically critical thinking, "cannot be profitably taught" in isolation from specific subjects because "critical thinking is not a general skill." My reason for asserting that CT is not a general skill was, again, that there are logically distinct types of thinking (e.g., mathematical, scientific, moral, etc.) which have standards and criteria that are *sui generis*. Thus, Siegel's valid observation that thinking can itself be an object of our thought, does not refute my point about the *sui generis* nature of the different kinds of thinking. Hence, the general pedagogical point remains intact as well.

Siegel's additional argument in this connection, which follows on from the first, is designed to show that "thinking" can, and should, be considered a general skill with a general range of application. He argues:

It is not the case that the general activity of thinking is logically connected to an X, any more than the general activity of cycling is logically connected to any particular bicycle. It is true that any given act of cycling must be done on some bicycle or other. But it surely does not follow that the general activity of cycling cannot be discussed independently of any particular bicycle. Indeed, we can state, and teach people, general skills of cycling (e.g., "Lean to the left when turning left" . . . etc.), even though instantiating these maneuvers and so exhibiting mastery of the general skills requires some particular bicycle. As with cycling, so with thinking . . . As we can teach cycling, so we can teach thinking.

It seems that this analogy with cycling falls wide of its mark for one crucial reason: "cycling" does denote a specific skill, where "thinking" does not. All manner of things can and do count as effective *thinking*, but not all manner of things can count as effective *cycling*. Cycling has a rather limited, if not unique, set of standards and criteria which determine what counts as effective cycling. But there is no similar set of finite criteria which determine (or define) effective thinking. Furthermore, Siegel keeps using the awkward phrase "the general activity of cycling," and this locution hides an important confusion: cycling is not a "general activity" but rather a specific one. The only sense in which it is general is that you can go different places, and for different purposes, but cycling, *qua* cycling, is a specific activity. Different destinations and purposes do not change the specific nature of the skill of cycling. But different problems and purposes do change the inherent nature of the skills required in thinking. No one set of skills can encompass "thinking," but one set of skills does encompass cycling.

Furthermore, in order to teach someone to be an effective cyclist, one specific bicycle is sufficient. But to teach someone to be an effective thinker (whatever that might mean), one specific thought or, indeed, type of thought is not sufficient. I do not, therefore, believe that thinking can be effectively taught as if it were a specific skill (as cycling can).

The next point in Siegel's paper which I will briefly comment upon is his claim that

> there are readily identifiable reasoning skills which do not refer to any specific subject matter, which do apply to diverse situations, and which are in fact the sort of skill which courses in CT seek to develop. Skills such as identifying assumptions, tracing relationships between premises and conclusions, identifying standard fallacies, and so on do not require the identification of specific subject matters.

I have analyzed and discussed these kinds of skills at length, both in my book and in subsequent papers, so I shall not repeat myself here. But, very briefly, I have argued that phrases like "the ability to identify assumptions," "the ability to draw valid conclusions from premises," "the ability to define a problem," etc., are phrases which semantically masquerade as descriptions of general abilities, but upon analysis, none of them actually denotes a generalized ability. Rather, each phrase subsumes a wide variety of *different* instances under its rubric, such that no singular ability could account for its diverse range of achievements. Take, for example, "the ability to recognize underlying assumptions." That this is not a singular ability can be appreciated by considering the fact that to recognize an underlying assumption in mathematics requires a different set of skills and abilities from those required for recognizing them in a political dispute, which are different again from those required in a scientific dispute. Thus, the phrase "ability to recognize underlying assumptions" does not denote any singular uniform ability, but rather a wide variety of them. Assumptions are not all cut from the same cloth. And even trained logicians cannot (to use Siegel's phrase) "readily identify them" within the various domains of human knowledge. You can, of course, logically characterize assumptions for students, that is, tell them what an assumption *is,* but this logical knowledge will not enable them to discover the diverse assumptions in the various knowledge domains and contexts. In general, I think many people, including Siegel, are actually bewitched by the grammar of these phrases into thinking that they denote singular, teachable skills, and that these skills can be "readily" applied no matter what the subject matter or context. In actual practice, these phrases refer to a wide variety of skills, to which logicians (and sometimes ourselves) give a common nomenclature. But we should not think that these collective descriptions refer to a singular skill.

Having said this, I should also point out (as Siegel has observed) that I do not regard the study of logic as totally without point. There is certainly something to be said for understanding what an assumption is, what a deductive inference is, etc. But I do object to such understandings being cashed out as providing general "critical thinking skill." Anyone generally familiar with the critical thinking literature knows that this is not merely a paranoid worry on my part. Though not his intent, perhaps, Siegel's interpretation of these general phrases as describing "general abilities" inadvertently provides aid and comfort to the army of false advertisers out there. Knowing what an assumption is, and knowing what a valid argument is, are far from sufficient to enable people to engage in effective critical thinking, at least in any significant context. In a sense, the study of logic is a bit like the study of formal linguistics by people who are about to study a foreign language: it is perhaps interesting, has some relevance, but it is largely beside the *practical* point.

Siegel now goes on to challenge my view that "reflective skepticism" forms a part of CT. He argues:

> Notice first that the notion of "reflective skepticism" is opaque. A skeptic might be reflective, and yet her skepticism unjustified. And it will not do to

justify skepticism in terms of its appropriateness, such appropriateness being determined by disciplinary or problem-area criteria, for often it is just those criteria which one needs to be reflectively skeptical about.

Two brief comments about this. First, I myself have pointed out, in my book and elsewhere, that the critical thinker often needs to challenge or query the foundations of certain domains of knowledge. Indeed, I have argued that such challenges constitute paradigm cases of CT. So Siegel sets up something of a straw man here. Furthermore, any effective or sensible challenges of this sort (e.g., challenging foundations) usually requires that the person knows quite a bit about the domain.

With respect to Siegel's point that "a skeptic might be reflective, and yet her skepticism unjustified," I agree entirely. I have been at pains to point out that CT is both a *task* and an *achievement* concept. There is nothing in the notion of CT which guarantees its own success. People sometimes try and fail at it. And there are cases where skepticism is unjustified. Indeed, part of what is involved in coming to understand a field or subject area is knowing when skepticism might be called for— even about the foundations or assumptions of that area. This is precisely why I call for an epistemological approach to CT—both within fields and about them. I see nothing "opaque" in this.

The longest single discussion in Siegel's paper has to do with the "relations of logic to CT." In my book I have argued that the informal logic movement (ILM) overestimates the role of logic in CT. In particular, I argued that the business of *reason assessment* is primarily an epistemic enquiry, since it has to do with truth, evidence, and beliefs. And logic, as such, has little (and often no) role to play in such endeavors. Siegel, on the other hand, wants to make a case that a subject-neutral logic plays a much larger role in reason assessment than I acknowledge.

Parenthetically, it is ironic that Siegel chides me here for not being absolutely clear about whether I hold that logic is *never* relevant to reason assessment, or only *sometimes,* or what. Consider, however, the "forthright" position he takes on this same question (*contra* me):

> Even if many, or even most, reasons are properly assessed only with reference to subject-specific criteria, *some* (and perhaps *many* or *most*) reasons are properly assessed *at least partially* in accordance with subject-neutral logical reasons.

And Siegel thinks that I was unclear about the precise role of logic in reason assessment! His own added qualifiers here have practically stripped his position from containing any real opposition to my view. To be honest, however, I think we have both "chickened out" of this thorny issue; because it involves making estimates (or guesses) as to how much, or how often, logic is required in everyday contexts. I have argued that it is not very often, and he has argued that it is quite a bit.

In any case, my position is that reason assessment, *per se,* is primarily an epistemic matter (not a logical one), because reasons are the premises *within* arguments which we must assess for their truth or plausibility. And when we are assessing the truth or plausibility of premises, we are engaged in an *epistemic* and not a *logical* endeavor. However, Siegel believes that more often than not (?) logic itself plays a substantial role in the assessment of reasons *per se.* He says:

> The fallacies furnish obvious examples here. To take just one: when Jehovah's Witnesses come to my door, and argue that I should believe in the divinity of the Bible because (for the reason that) the Bible proclaims itself to be the divine word of God, it does not take a theological or other subject-specific information or criteria to realize that the reason offered does not in fact support the claim it is offered in support of. Rather, it begs the question. Here logic *is* to reason assessment.

Even in this example, however, which is offered as a clear-cut case of logic assessing reason, I would insist to the contrary that the assessment of the reason given is still epistemic rather than logical. If you examine the reason given by the Jehovah's Witnesses, you will see that the reason given does (however weakly) support the conclusion that the Bible has divine origin. Indeed, we should be surprised if the Bible did *not* assert of itself that it has divine origin. Of course, we would not believe this grand assertion simply for that reason, but it does constitute *some* evidence (however weak) for its divine origin. We remain skeptical of the assertion because we would want other corroborative evidence of some kind which would help support the authenticity or veracity of the assertion; without such we must remain skeptical. But notice that our skepticism is based upon *epistemic,* not logical, considerations having to do with what constitutes good reasons for this claim. If, in a parallel example, the FBI received a letter which read: "I, John Doe, do hereby confess that I am the authentic assassin of Jimmy Hoffa, etc., etc.," the FBI would and should take this as *some* evidence of the claim asserted in the letter. The same holds for the Bible case. In both, we are assessing the veracity or authenticity of evidence (albeit weak); but *logic* does not reveal the weakness of such evidence. Thus, I still regard epistemology, and not logic, as the major tool of reason assessment. What has gone wrong in the ILM generally, and to a lesser extent in Siegel's paper, is that both seriously *underestimate* the complexity of ordinary information or knowledge and they seriously *overestimate* the role of logic in helping to unravel such complexity.

Siegel also argues that since deductive formal logic provides a kind of "ideal type" of good argumentation, it therefore constitutes "a crucial component of an adequate conception of CT." Hence, it is essential that formal logic be taught as at least part of CT courses. However, we can all think of cases of very bright people, whom we would regard as good critical thinkers, who have never even heard of formal logic, much less studied it. Such cases clearly show that the study of formal logic is not necessary for effective critical thinking. Thus, despite the intrinsic merit of formal logic, which is considerable, it is a mistake to treat it as either necessary or sufficient for critical thinking.

And finally, Siegel challenges and rejects my claim that CT is a dimension, or subset, of rationality generally. He claims that CT and rationality are "coextensive" and "equivalent." He says:

> The distinction McPeck draws here between CT and rationality is untenable . . . If McPeck is to maintain his "epistemological" or "good reasons" approach to CT, then he must reject the limitation he seems to want to place on the range of CT in his distinction between CT and rationality. The reason assessment component of CT extends to the assessment of all reasons, not just "meta-reasons" concerning the constitution, relevance or appropriateness of problematic "ground floor" reasons.
>
> Once one rejects this limitation on the range of CT, the distinction between CT and rationality collapses. CT is coextensive with rationality not merely a dimension of it, for rationality is "coextensive" with the relevance of reasons," as is CT. The connection between rationality and reasons is as tight as it can be.

I have two comments to make about this position. First, I would argue that the concept of "rationality" is not only broader than "CT," but it is also broader than "reason assessment." Thus, contrary to Siegel, it is not coextensive nor equivalent with either of them. Let's begin with "reason assessment." While the assessment of reasons (indeed, any kind of reason) can, in principle, be the object of rationality, it does not follow that rationality always consists in the assessment of reasons. Sometimes it is rational merely to accept certain reasons without assessing them. For example, it would be rational to merely accept directions to an address from a stranger when in a strange city (i.e., it's better than wondering). Also, I might rationally believe that it is going to rain this evening just because the weatherman said so. In neither of these rational actions is the assessment of reasons involved. While it is possible in principle to provide assessments of these reasons, the rational actions themselves do not involve such assessments: the reasons are here merely accepted. Thus, unless one is going to stretch the meaning of "reason assessment" beyond recognition, since there is no process of assessment going on here, I do not see how these rational actions could be seen as cases of "reason assessment."

Furthermore, consider the very large class of rational acts that we routinely engage in, sometimes even out of habit, where "reason assessment" plays no part. For example, when I use a calculator to do sums, I rationally rely upon it without questioning or thinking about whether its answers are correct. With more complex calculations, we might not even understand the reasons if they should be provided; yet we routinely, and rationally, rely on such things. But even in those cases where we were once provided with reasons which we understood, we do not continue to assess those reasons each time. Indeed, to the contrary, it would be considered irrational to do so. Even when I brush my teeth, which is now a rational habit (just as smoking is an irrational habit), I seldom rehearse the reasons why it is rational. But it is nonetheless rational for that. Therefore, not all cases of rationality are cases of "reason assessment." And, *a fortiori,* not all cases of rationality involve CT. My position is, and has been, that CT and reason assessment are a subclass of rationality. Therefore, they are not equivalent or coextensive notions, as Siegel argues.

Second, my analysis of the concept of CT as "the disposition and skill to engage in an activity with reflective skepticism" specifically tried to capture this particular dimension of rationality, and to set CT off from the other kinds of rational behavior. I believe this partitioning is consistent with the way we talk about CT in our daily language, and with our preanalytical intuitions about CT. Just as we, and our language, recognize that not all cases of thinking are cases of CT, we also recognize that not all cases of rational behavior are cases of CT. To argue, as Siegel does, that rationality is coextensive with CT not only flies in the face of ordinary language, but it leaves one to defend the view that brushing one's teeth is an instance of CT.

CHAPTER 9

McPeck's mistakes

Richard Paul

Most educational commentators and most of the general public seem to agree on at least one thing: the schools are in deep trouble. Many graduates, at all levels, are characterized as lacking the abilities to read, write, and think with a minimal level of clarity, coherence, and critical/ analytic exactitude. Most commentators agree as well that a significant part of the problem is a pedagogical diet excessively rich in memorization and superficial rote performance and insufficiently rich in, if not devoid of, autonomous critical thought. This complaint is not entirely new in American education, but the degree of concern and the growing but quiet revolution represented by those attempting to meet that concern is worthy of note. (A recent ERIC computer search identified 1,849 articles in the last seven years with *critical thinking* as a major descriptor.[1] The roots of this multifaceted movement can be traced back in a number of directions, but one of the deepest and most important goes back as far as Ed Glaser's *Experiment in the Development of Critical Thinking* (1946). The manner in which this root of the movement has, after a halting start, progressively built up a head of steam, has been partially chronicled by Johnson and Blair.[2] It is now firmly established at the college and university level, where it affects an increasing number of courses that focus on "critical thinking" or "informal logic," courses designed to provide the kind of shot in the arm for critical thinking that general composition courses are expected to provide for writing.[3] The influence of this current in the movement is being increasingly felt at lower levels of education, but in a more variable, if somewhat less effective, way.

At this point enter John McPeck with his book *Critical Thinking and Education,* which promises us (on its dust jacket) "a timely critique of the major work in the field," "rigorous ideas on the proper place of critical thinking in the philosophy of education," and "a thorough analysis of what the concept is," as well as providing "a sound basis on which the role of critical thinking in the schools can be evaluated." The book is important, not only because it is the first to attempt a characterization of the recent critical thinking movement, but more so because the foundational mistakes it makes are uniquely instructive, mistakes so eminently reflective of "the spirit of the age" they are likely to show up in many more places than this book alone. Unfortunately, because of serious flaws in its theoretical underpinnings, the book doubtless will lead some of McPeck's readers down a variety of blind alleys, create unnecessary obstacles to some important programs being developed, and encourage some—not many, I hope— to dismiss the work of some central figures in the field (Scriven, D'Angelo, and Ennis, most obviously.) At the root of the problem is McPeck's (unwitting?) commitment to a rarefied form of logical (epistemological) atomism, a commitment which is essential if he is to rule out, as he passionately wants to, all general skills of thought and so to give himself *a priori* grounds to oppose every and all programs that try to develop or enhance such skills.

McPeck's "mistakes" are, from one vantage point, glaring and fundamental; from another they are seductive, and as I have suggested above, quite "natural." They bear examination from a number of points of view. Certainly there are few who would not see the fallacy in inferring that because one cannot write without writing about something, some specific subject or other, it is therefore unintelligible "muddled nonsense" to maintain general composition courses or to talk about general, as against subject-specific, writing skills. Likewise, most would think bizarre someone who argued that because speech requires something spoken about, it therefore is senseless to set up general courses in speech and incoherent to talk of *general* speaking skills.

Yet McPeck's keystone inference, logically parallel and equally fallacious in my view, is likely to be seductively attractive to many teachers and administrators in the form in which McPeck articulates it:

> It is a matter of conceptual truth that thinking is always thinking about X, and the X can never be "everything in general" but must always be something in particular. Thus, the claim "I teach my students to think" is at worst false and at best misleading.

> Thinking, then, is logically connected to an X. Since this fundamental point is reasonably easy to grasp, it is surprising that critical thinking should have become reified into a curriculum subject and the teaching of it an area of expertise of its own.

> In isolation, it neither refers to nor denotes any particular skill. It follows from this that it makes no sense to talk about critical thinking as a distinct subject and that it therefore cannot profitably be taught as such. To the extent that critical thinking is not about a specific subject X, it is both conceptually and practically empty. The statement "I teach critical thinking," *simpliciter,* is vacuous because there is no generalized skill properly called critical thinking. (Pp. 4 and 5)

Many would, I suspect, find it equally attractive to conclude with McPeck that "the real problem with uncritical students is not a deficiency in a general skill, such as logical ability, but rather a general lack of education in the traditional sense," and that "elementary schools are fully occupied with their efforts to impart the three R's together with the most elementary information about the world around them," and hence have no *time* to teach critical thinking as well. They might not be as comfortable with his notion that "there is nothing in the logic of education that requires that schools should engage in education," and "nothing contradictory in saying, 'This is a fine school, and I recommend it to others, even though it does not engage in education.' "

Still, this latter point is mentioned only once and not endlessly repeated in an array of different forms, as in his major refrain that "thinking of any kind is always about X." The "X" of this refrain, that to which McPeck believes the logic of all thought is to be relativized, is itself characterized in a litany of synonyms ("the question at issue," "the subject matter," "the parent field," "the field of research," "the specific performance," "the discipline," "the cognitive domain," and so forth), as are the various criteria (the need for "specialized and technical language," "technical information," "field-dependent concepts," "unique logic," "unique skills," "intra-field considerations," "subject-specific information," and so forth) imposed on the critical thinker by the X in question. The hypnotic effect of the continual reiteration of the truism implicit in his major refrain alongside a variety of formulations of his major conclusion is such that readers not used to slippery *non sequiturs* are apt to miss the logical gap *ex praemissis conclusio*.

If nothing else, the reader is bound to feel something of the attractiveness—in this technological/specialist world of ours—of McPeck's placing of critical thought squarely in the center of an atomistic, information-centered model of knowledge. We are already comfortable with the notion that to learn is to amass large quantities of specialized or erudite facts, and we know that facts are of different *types*. We tend, in other words, to think of knowledge on the model of the computers we are so enamored of: on the one hand, a huge mass of atomic facts (our data bank), and on the other, a specific set of categories—McPeck's logical domains—which organize them into higher-order generalizations by formulas and decision-procedures requiring technical information about the facts to be manipulated. Critical thought in this context requires understanding both the data bank and the established procedures.

But it is well to remember that we cannot ask computers multicategorical questions, especially those kinds that cut across the disciplines in such a way as to require reasoned perspective on the data from a "global" point of view. Such questions, structuring the very warp and woof of everyday life, are typically dialectical, settled, that is, by *general* canons of argument, by objection (from one point of view) and reply (from another), by case and countercase, by debate not only about the answer to the question but also about the very logic of the question itself. Most social and world problems are of this nature, as well as those that presuppose the subject's worldview. For example, consider those social problems that call for a judgment of the equity of the distribution of wealth and power, of the "causes" of poverty, of the justification and limits of welfare, of the nature or existence of the military-industrial complex, of the value or danger of capitalism, of the character of racism and sexism or their history and manifestations, of the nature of communism or socialism, etc. The position we take on any one of these issues is likely to reflect our conception of human nature (the extent of human "equality" and what "follows" from it as so conceived, the nature and causes of human "laziness" and "ambition"), the need for "social change" or "conservatism," even the character of the "cosmos" and "nature."

This point was brought home to me recently when I got into a lengthy disagreement with an acquaintance on the putative "justification" of the American invasion of Grenada. Before long we were discussing questions of morality, the appropriate interpretation of international law, supposed rights of countries to defend their interests, spheres of influence, the character of U.S. and Soviet foreign policy, the history of the two countries, the nature and history of the CIA, the nature of democracy, whether it can exist without elections, who has credibility, how to judge it, the nature of the media, how to assess it, whether it reflects an "American" party line, sociocentrism, our own personalities, consistency, etc. Especially illuminating and instructive was the distinctive pattern that these discussions took. It was eminently clear that we disagreed in our respective worldviews, our global perspectives. Because we each conceived of the world with something like an integrated point of view, we conceptualized the problem and its elements differently. Specialized information was differently interpreted by us. There were no discipline-specific skills to save the day.

McPeck avoids commenting on such problems except insofar as they presuppose specialized information, on which he then focuses. From a logical atomist's point of view (everything to be carefully placed in an appropriate *sui generis* logical category, there to be settled by appropriate specialists in that category), dialectical, multicategorical questions are anomalous. When noticed, the tendency is to try to fabricate specialized categories for them or to break them down into a summary complex of monocategorical elements. Hence, the problem of peace in relation to the military-industrial complex would be broken down by atomists into discrete sets of economic, social, ethical, historical, and psychological problems, or what have you, each to be analyzed and settled discretely. This neat and tidy picture of the world of knowledge as a specialist's world is the Procrustean bed that McPeck has prepared for critical thought. To aspire to critical thought, on this view, is to recognize that it can be achieved only within narrow confines of one's life ("There are no Renaissance men in this age of specialized knowledge," p. 7). It is possible only in those dimensions where one can function as a "properly

trained physicist, historian . . . [or] art critic" (p. 150), etc., and so
learn specialized knowledge and unique skills.

McPeck identifies the bogey man in critical thinking in a variety of
ways ("the logic approach," "formalism," "informal logic," "naive logical positivism," "logic *simpliciter,*" and so forth), but the bulk of his
book is spent in attacking scholars associated with the Informal Logic
Movement (Ennis, Johnson, Blair, D'Angelo, and Scriven). The general
charge against them is, predictably, that they have failed to grasp what
follows from the logic of the concept of critical thinking—that it is
"muddled nonsense" to base it on general skills—and that such misguided attempts necessarily result in "the knee-jerk application of skills"
and "superficial opinion masquerading as profound insight," and are
thus bound to run aground.

Since McPeck rests so much on his conceptual analysis, it is appropriate to note what he leaves out of it. He does not consider the full
range of uses of the word *critical* as they are relevant to various everyday
senses of the predicate "thinks critically." He does not consider the
history of critical thought, the various theories of it implicit in the
work of Plato, Aristotle, Kant, Hegel, Marx, Freud, Weber, Sartre,
Habermas, and so forth. He does not consider the implications of such
classic exemplars as Socrates, Voltaire, Rousseau, Thomas Paine, Henry
David Thoreau, or even of an H. L. Mencken or Ivan Illich, to mention
a few that come to mind—whether, that is, their critical thinking can or
cannot be explained by, or reduced to, specialized knowledge or domain-
specific skills. He does not consider the rich range of programs that have
been developed in the recent work in the field (he has it in mind that in
principle there *cannot* be a field of research here). He does not consider
the possibility that in the light of the rich variety of programs, reflecting
somewhat different emphases, interests, priorities, it may be premature
to attempt to pin down in a few words "the concept of critical thinking."
He does not consider the possibility that the scholars he is criticizing
may be using the term in an *inductive* sense, hence not presupposing or
claiming a definitive analysis of the concept, but restricting their focus
rather to some of its necessary, not sufficient, conditions (for example:
aiding students in developing greater skill in identifying and formulating
questions at issue, distinguishing evidence from conclusion, isolating
conceptual problems and problems of credibility, recognizing "common"
fallacies, and coming to a clearer sense of what a claim or an assumption
or an inference or an implication is, and so forth).

One result is that his analysis of "the concept of critical thinking" is
in all essentials completed in the first thirteen pages of the book, with
his foundational inference in place by page 4. Another is that he gives
a most unsympathetic and at times highly misleading representation of
most of those he critiques (Ennis, Glaser, D'Angelo, Johnson, Blair,
and Scriven).

In order to have space to develop the broader implications of McPeck's analysis, I will illustrate this latter tendency solely with respect to Robert Ennis, who is at the center of most of his critical remarks in chapter 3, "The Prevailing View of the Concept of Critical Thinking." McPeck introduces this chapter with three interrelated general charges about the "theoretical foundation" of the prevailing concept: that those who hold it subscribe "to the verifiability criterion of meaning," are "marked by a naive form of logical positivism," and have "an unquestioned faith in the efficacy of science and its methods to settle every significant controversy requiring critical thought." However, nowhere in the chapter does he back up these charges. And I myself do not find anything in the work of Ennis (or of D'Angelo for that matter) that suggests such a theoretical commitment.

McPeck focuses his critique on Ennis's article "A Concept of Critical Thinking," published in 1962, despite the fact that Ennis has been regularly publishing and modifying his position to date. Second, it is clear that Ennis, even in this early article, does not take himself to be providing a definitive analysis of the concept; he offers but a "truncated" working definition. He describes his article as providing a "range definition" which has "vague boundaries," based on an examination of "the literature on goals of the schools and the literature on the criterion of good thinking," and designed merely to "select" "those aspects" which come under the notion of critical thinking as "the correct assessing of statements." He makes it clear that he is leaving out at least one crucial element ("the judging of value statement is deliberately excluded"). He makes clear that his working definition does not settle the question as to how best to teach critical thinking, e.g., whether as a separate subject or within subject areas. Finally, it is clear that he is concerned with critical thinking as an open-ended and complicated set of processes that can be set out in analyzed form only for the purpose of theoretical convenience, a list of "aspects" and "dimensions" that can be learned "at various levels."[4]

McPeck's motive for critiquing Ennis's concept is clearly the fact that Ennis does not define critical thinking so as to link it "conceptually with particular activities and special fields of knowledge" (p. 56). And because McPeck sees this conceptual link as necessary, as given *in* the concept, it is, in his view, "impossible to conceive of critical thinking as a generalized skill" (p. 56). In other words, Ennis is conceiving of critical thinking in an "impossible" and therefore incoherent, muddled, and contradictory way. If we are not persuaded of this conceptual link and read Ennis to be making more modest claims than McPeck attributes to him, most of McPeck's criticisms fall by the wayside.

Let us look more closely then at McPeck's model and its implications. It depends upon the plausibility of placing any line of thought into a "category," "domain," "subject area," or "field," which placement provides, implicitly or explicitly, criteria for judging in that line of thought. It tacitly assumes that all thinking is in one and only one category, that we can, without appealing to an expert on experts, tell what the appropriate category is, and thus what specialized information or skills are unique to it. Each discrete category creates the possibility for specialized concepts, experience, skills, etc., and for some limited set of people to develop the necessary wherewithal to think critically within it. Since there is a large number of logical domains and we can be trained only in a few of them, it follows that we must use our critical judgment mainly to suspend judgment and/or to defer to experts when we ourselves are not expert. It leaves little room for the classical concept of the liberally educated person as having skills of learning that are general and not domain-specific. It is worthwhile therefore to set out more particularly, if somewhat abstractly, why it is unacceptable.

First of all, the world is not given to us sliced up into logical categories, and there is not one, but an indefinitely large number of ways in which we may "divide" it, that is, experience, perceive, or think about the world, and no "detached" point of view from the supreme perspective of which we can decide on the appropriate taxonomy for the "multiple realities" of our lives. Conceptual schemes create logical domains, and it is human thought, not nature, that creates them.

Second, our conceptual schemes themselves can be classified in an indefinitely large number of ways. To place a line of reasoning into a category and so to identify it by its "type" is heuristic, not ontological. Even concepts and lines of reasoning *clearly* within one category are also simultaneously within others. Most of what we say and think, to put it another way, is not only open- but *multi*textured as well. For example, in what logical domain does the (technical?) concept of alcoholism solely belong: disease, addiction, crime, moral failing, cultural pattern, lifestyle choice, defect of socialization, self-comforting behavior, psychological escape, personal weakness . . . ? How many points of view can be used to illuminate it? Then, is each of them *in* one or many categories?

Not only conceptualizing "things," but most especially classifying what we have conceptualized, are not matters about which we can give the final word to experts and specialists. To place something said or thought into a category, from the perspective of which we intend to judge it, is to take a potentially contentious position with respect to it. There are no specialists who have the definitive taxonomy or undebatable means for so deciding. The category a thing is in is logically dependent upon what it is *like,* but all things (including conceptual schemes) are like any number of other things (other conceptual schemes for example) in any number of ways and so are *in,* dependent on our purposes, any number of logical domains.

Consider for example Copernicus's statements about the earth in relation to the sun. These are, you may be tempted to say, astronomical statements and nothing else. But if they become a part of concepts and lines of thought that have radically reoriented philosophical, social, religious, economic, and personal thought, as indeed they have, are they *merely in* that one category? When we begin to think in a cross-categorical way, as the intellectual heirs of Copernicus, Darwin, Freud, and Marx, are there category-specific skills and specialists to interpret that thought and tell us what the correct synthesis of these ingredients is and how it ought to color or guide our interpretation or critical assessment of statements "within" some particular domain or other?

The most important place that knowledge has in any lives is, on my view, that of shaping our concept of things *überhaupt,* our system of values, meanings, and interpretive schemes. This is the domain in which critical thought is most important to us. We spend only a small percentage of our lives making judgments as specialists, and even then we typically give a broader meaning to those acts as persons and citizens. Hence, a business person may place a high value on her professional acts as contributing to the social good. She may interpret and assess the schools and education on the model of a business. She may judge the political process in its relation to the business community and see business opportunities and freedom as conceptually interrelated. She may then unfavorably judge societies not organized so as to favor "free investment of capital" as dangerous threats to human well-being, and make other such judgments. Logical synthesis, cutting across categories, exacting metaphors from one domain and using them to organize others, arguing for or against the global metaphors of others—are intellectual acts that are grounded ultimately not in the criteria and skills of specialists, not in some science or other or any combination thereof, but in the art of thinking of anything in its "right" relationship to things *überhaupt.*

Hence, if we are to be rational agents, we must learn to think critically about how we "totalize" our experience and bring that total picture to bear on particular dimensions of our lives. We cannot, without losing our autonomy, delegate the construction of those crucial acts to specialists or technicians. Students, teachers, and persons in general need to maintain their critical autonomy even in—especially in—the face of specialists and even with respect to claims made within specialized areas. If democracy is a viable form of government and way of life, then judgments not only of policy but of worldview are the common task of all, not the prerogative of privileged groups of specialists. We need to pay special attention to those *general* skills of critical cross-examination, for they are what enable us to maintain our autonomous judgment in the midst of experts. These payoff skills, of civic literacy and personal autonomy, can be articulated best not in "procedures" that read like a technical manual but in "principles" that will often sound platitudinous or have the ring of "general" advice. Platitudes, however, can become insights definitive of general skills when systematic case-by-case practice is supported by careful argument for and against. It is a platitude to say, for example, that the press and the media of a nation tend to cover the news so as to foster or presuppose the correctness of the "worldview" of that nation or its government. But this bit of "common knowledge" is a far cry from the very important general skill of reading a newspaper so as to note how, where, and when it is insinuating nationalistic biases. Or again, it is one thing to recognize that all "news" is news from a point of view. It is another thing to be able to read or hear it with the critical sensitivity that enables one to see one point of view presupposed and others ruled out. McPeck thinks otherwise.

> Where there is only common knowledge, there can only be common criticism—which is usually plain enough for one and all to see. This view not only represents a very shallow, or superficial, understanding of the cognitive ingredients of critical thinking, but it is also forced to underestimate and play down the real complexities that usually underlie even apparently "common" or "everyday" problems. The solutions to "common," "everyday" problems, if they are in fact problems, are seldom common or everyday. In any event, the educational aspirations of our schools are (fortunately) set higher than the treatment of issues that could otherwise be solved by common sense. Where common sense cannot solve a problem, one quickly finds the need for subject-specific information; hence, the traditional justification for subject-oriented courses. (Pp. 156–57)

In my view, the logics we use, and which we are daily constructing and reconstructing, are far more mutable, less discrete, more general, more open and multitextured, more social, more dialectical, and even more personal—and hence far less susceptible to domain-specific skills and concepts—than McPeck dares to imagine. We need to base our model of the critical thinker not on the domain-bound individual with subject-specific skills, but on the disciplined generalist. This means that we ought to encourage the student as soon as possible to recognize that in virtually every area of our lives, cutting across categories every which way, there are multiple conflicting viewpoints and theories vying for our allegiance, the possible truth of virtually all of which calls for shifts in our global perspective. The general skills necessary to finding our way about this dialectical world are more appropriately captured in the work of an Ennis, D'Angelo, or a Scriven than in that of a McPeck. *General* critical skills and dispositions cannot be learned without content, without doubt, but few would disagree with this point, certainly not Ennis, D'Angelo, or Scriven. The real and pressing question is not whether content is necessary to thought (it is), but whether "content" restricts us to thinking "within" as against "across" and "between" and "beyond" categories. If there is such a thing as having a global perspective, and if that perspective not only sets out categories but also their taxonomy, and if such a perspective can be assessed only by appeal to general dialectical skills, not domain- or subject-specific ones, then McPeck's vision of critical thinking instruction is fundamentally flawed and the move to a greater emphasis on critical thinking in education is more challenging, and to some perhaps more threatening, than has generally been recognized up to now.[5]

CHAPTER 10

Richard Paul's critique of
Critical Thinking and Education
John E. McPeck

Usually, it is unwise for an author of a book even to attempt responding to a published critique of his/her book with a brief rebuttal. He/she is always on the defense, and cannot, therefore, avoid appearing defensive. An essay in the *New York Review of Books* recently described all such attempted rebuttals as an "ABM": Author's Big Mistake. (I can recall one rare, but notable, exception to this general caution. It is from the famous Leibniz-Clarke correspondence, wherein Leibniz prudently responded to a lengthy and bitter critique by Clarke with but one statement: "I deny the major premise." Anything more is likely to become an ABM.)

In the present case, the editors of *Informal Logic* have kindly requested that I respond to Richard Paul's review of my *Critical Thinking and Education*. And they have specifically asked that I not review this review, but rather restrict myself to the "substantive philosophical differences between us." With this restriction in mind, therefore, I hope it becomes clear that my comments are not intended to rebut all of Paul's many charges. It is rather an attempt to uncover what I think he has gotten wrong, and to discuss the "substantive philosophical differences between us." Putting the ABM aside, my intent is to generate light, not heat.

I will treat each of Paul's more substantive points in their order of appearance.

Paul's opening comment about my book asserts that I made several "foundational mistakes," and that these have "serious flaws in their theoretical underpinnings." Little doubt the book might contain some of this. But as I examine Paul's critique, I find less evidence of "mistakes" and "serious flaws" than of misunderstanding of my position and perhaps genuine disagreement.

The first, and perhaps most pervasive, "mistake" that Paul finds is that I supposedly subscribe to "a rarefied form of logical atomism." It is never quite clear to me what, precisely, Paul means by logical atomism. His meaning clearly differs from what most philosophers understand by that phrase, namely, the basic language elements in Wittgenstein's *Tractatus*. Nor is his meaning at all like Russell's meaning in *The Philosophy of Logical Atomism* (1918). Rather, Paul seems to be coining his own phrase, which is apparently meant to refer to my view that not all knowledge and skills are cut from the same cloth. It is quite true that I defend the view that, for example, a critical mathematician possesses a kind of knowledge and skill that are different from those of a critical historian. And, in general, different domains of knowledge have (more often than not) characteristically different patterns of reasoning and argument that are peculiar to themselves. This view, incidentally, is a well-trodden philosophical path which leads back to Aristotle's *Posterior Analytics,* or Wittgenstein's *Philosophical Investigations,* particularly the notion of different "language games." Thus, while my particular statement of my position may or may not contain certain errors, it is, I think, gross overstatement to claim that the view contains "serious flaws in its theoretical underpinnings," or that it consists of serious "foundational mistakes." Aristotle, Wittgenstein, and I (if you'll forgive me) may all be wrong of course, but if so, it is not as obvious as Paul seems to think.

The major philosophical differences that divide Paul and me seem to reside in his basic charge that my position is "atomistic," or "technological/specialist," as he sometimes calls it. However, it seems to me that this charge is based upon both a misinterpretation of my view, and also an honest disagreement. At times, I confess, I'm not sure which is which, but let me try to explain these differences as succinctly as I can.

Paul marshals two separate and distinguishable arguments to support his charge (or characterization) of my position as being "atomistic" or "technological/specialist." The first argument concerns my rejection of generalized reasoning skills, and the second reflects his observation that most problems are in fact "multicategorical" and not domain-specific. Both of these arguments, however, are simply two different ways of rejecting my general view that critical thinking and rationality are *primarily* domain-specific and context-dependent (therefore, they do not represent "general reasoning skills," in Paul's desired sense). I will treat each of Paul's arguments in a moment, but I think there is a much larger problem that exacerbates our disagreement. This larger problem cannot be resolved here, but I think it important to recognize that it does exist and that it helps explain the nature of our disagreement.

As time goes on, it becomes increasingly clear to me that my differences with the Informal Logic Movement (ILM), generally, may have their roots in a fundamentally different conception of how logic and language are connected to thought. This fundamental difference amounts to nothing less than a Kuhn-type paradigm clash about the nature of these connections. Thus, we continue to talk past one another, like ships passing in the night, each failing to be persuaded by the other's arguments. This paradigm clash is between what I would call a Wittgensteinian view about the nature of logic, language and thought that stresses the semantic and pragmatic features of logic, and the more typically North American view which stresses the formal, syntactical features of logic and reasoning. For Wittgenstein, logic inheres *within* language and speech acts themselves. In the logicist (or North American view), logic is an exogenous system of rules and principles into which language can be plugged as a variable. While informal logic is less mathematical, or less formal, than formal logic, nonetheless it shares the same syntactic preoccupation with *rules* and *principles* of reasoning (of a weaker sort) that is so characteristic of formal logic proper. (Hence, the persistent talk about "theories of fallacy," "theories of reasoning," "theories of informal logic," etc., all of which seek *generalizable* canons of reasoning and argument in one form or other.)

Wittgenstein, on the other hand, did not believe such canons of reasoning were forthcoming, because the locus of logic (not mathematical or formal, however) resides within the speech acts themselves. For Wittgenstein, you can no more separate the *logic* of a speech act from the act itself than you can separate all the thread from the cloth and still have the cloth. To the extent that this view might be true incidentally, it helps to explain the well-known difficulties associated with trying to accurately portray the true structure of real arguments with formal schemata—the more real the argument, the more difficult is the portrayal. Wittgenstein's view explains why this is so. I am not trying to defend Wittgenstein, but merely to point out that when "logic" and "reasoning" are perceived from these fundamentally different points of view, much confusion and misunderstanding is bound to ensue.

I first saw evidence of this basic clash at the *First International Symposium on Informal Logic* (University of Windsor, 1978), when Peter A. Minkus presented a paper from an avowedly Wittgensteinian point of view. (Its title was "Arguments That Aren't Arguments.") Despite the paper's unusual style and at times confusing presentation, the amount of misunderstanding (and hostility) which it generated far surpassed any internal muddles it may have contained. The two paradigms had come face-to-face: neither understood the other. Further evidence of this clash can be found in Ralph Johnson's painstaking review of Stephen Toulmin's *Introduction to Reasoning* in *Informal Logic* (March 1981). In his bones, Toulmin is a Wittgensteinian, and he views logic from this perspective. But in *Introduction to Reasoning* he is trying to have it both ways by straddling the two paradigms: he is trying to fit a Wittgensteinian view of logic, and logical relationships, into a semiformalistic mold. Needless to say, the fit is a very awkward one at best—as square pegs into round holes always are. Johnson, indeed, has done a fair and credible job showing the several ways in which Toulmin has failed in his objective. However, Johnson's yardstick for measuring success or failure was a typically *formalistic* (e.g., North American) one. Toulmin's program simply does not square with formalistic *desiderata,* as Johnson correctly points out; but the later Wittgenstein would have predicted as much.

The paradigm clash between Toulmin and Johnson is at its clearest in Johnson's discussion of Toulmin's key notion of a "warrant," which is intended to displace rules of inference. Johnson writes:

> Of all the elements in Toulmin's schema, the warrant is the one I have the greatest problem understanding. The intuitive idea seems clear enough, but (as I will try to show) Toulmin's rather breezy style of exposition creates some of the confusion. Then, too, this is the element that departs most radically from the traditional schema, thereby forcing one to look at the structure of arguments in a different light. That takes some getting used to. (P. 21)

Johnson also adds revealingly: "The problem is thorny enough to make one hanker for the rarefied climes of formal logic—almost!"

The "problem of understanding" which Johnson has with Toulmin's schema is, I submit, not simply a matter of incomplete comprehension that one might find between two informal logicians. It is, rather, a classic paradigm clash between two people who hold radically different views about the nature of the connection between logic, language, and thought. Such deep-rooted differences cannot be resolved by simply cleaning up a few terms like *warrant* or *ground,* because these concepts have no equivalent meaning in the other paradigm. They are part of a different philosophical network.

I might say that I share Johnson's dissatisfaction with Toulmin's notion of "warrants"; it is woolly. However, I also share Toulmin's basic view about the nature of the connections between logic, language and thought (which is Wittgensteinian.) This view, therefore, puts me in the other paradigm.

I think this difference helps to explain: (a) much of the deeper misunderstandings about my view; and (b) why my view seems to appear so *a priori* to some folks, including Richard Paul. It is interesting, incidentally, that in Great Britain, where my book was first published, my general position has been received with polite yawns, since it is there more or less commonplace. (This, of course, does not mean it is correct; but it does mean it is *understood.*) Enough, however, about this fundamental difference. It cannot be resolved here. But I think it important to recognize that it exists.

Back to Paul's two arguments as promised. The first, you will recall, has to do with my rejection of generalized reasoning skills, which Paul uses to support his general charge about my view being "atomistic" or "technological/specialist." With the possible exception of general intelligence (or IQ), I *do* deny generalized reasoning skills. Or, at least, we have not discovered any thus far (psychologists included). This rejection, however, does not entail nor suggest a "technological/specialist" view of human reasoning, as Paul implies. To say, as I do, that the various broad domains of human understanding (e.g., math, literature, science, morality) require different kinds of concepts, skills, and patterns of reasoning peculiar to themselves and are not generalizable across domains, is *not* to insist that people must be "specialists," as such, in any particular area. It is rather, to point out that the particular ingredients of rationality and critical thinking are less generic and more idiosyncratic than any single set of generalized reasoning skills can capture, namely, the so-called critical thinking skills. In my view, to become rational one must come to understand the different logical, conceptual, and epistemic differences that obtain between the different kinds of questions and problems that there are (e.g., mathematical, scientific, philosophic, artistic, moral, etc.). When one clearly understands these logical differences, one comes to appreciate the different procedures (or methods) that might be appropriate for answering (and asking) questions in these domains. This, indeed, is precisely the kind of understanding which a liberal education attempts to provide. And it is a kind of understanding and preparation for critical thinking that I have repeatedly advocated in my book, and several other papers. Whatever else a liberal education is, it is not "technological/specialistic." Indeed, it is often criticized from some quarters (e.g., business) precisely because it does not provide enough specialized knowledge. It should not go unnoticed, by the way, that training in specific "reasoning skills" is far more specialized than anything that I could have advocated. Thus the irony in the charge of "technological/specialist."

Paul argues that my rejection of generalized reasoning skills is a *non sequitur* because, he argues, that it does not follow from the fact that thought requires a specific object X (to be thought *about*) that there are no generalized reasoning skills. To show how "bizarre" he thinks this reasoning is, he attempts to draw analogies with general writing skills (or "composition") and "general speaking skills":

> Likewise most would think bizarre someone who argued that because speech requires something specific spoken about, it, therefore, is senseless to set up general courses in speech and incoherent to talk of *general* speaking skills.

But let us be very clear about something. I am *not* engaged in an analysis of "writing," nor of "speaking": I am engaged in an analysis of "thinking," which is an entirely different concept. It *might* make sense to talk about "general writing skills" and perhaps "general speaking skills," but it does not follow from this (as Paul implies) that it makes similar sense to talk of "general thinking skills." There are people who can think, for example, but cannot write, just as there are people who can think but cannot speak. One would, therefore, expect things to be true of "writing" and "speaking" which might not be true of "thinking." Notice, for example, that we do sometimes say of someone that "he doesn't know what he is *talking* about," but it would be odd to assert that "he doesn't know what he is *thinking* about." Thinking and speaking are simply different concepts, and they refer to different kinds of tasks.

I would, moreover, point out that even in writing and in speaking, the major portion of the task consists in having knowledge of what it is, specifically, that one is trying to write or speak *about*. As every teacher knows (particularly "composition" teachers), a student cannot write intelligently about something he does not understand. Clear understanding is a necessary condition for clear writing— infinite monkeys and typewriters notwithstanding. The same for speaking. Frankly, I have always been a touch dubious about general speech courses, such as those Paul mentions. Unless their point is, as with Dale Carnegie courses, to somehow spruce up delivery or elocution, I see little point to them. Because, in the end, what good speaking consists in is understanding *what* you are speaking about—and general speech courses cannot deliver this understanding. If Paul is suggesting that "general reasoning" courses make about as much sense as "general speech" courses, then I agree with him.

One final point. If thinking is always about something (e.g., some X), as I have suggested, then "critical thinking" *per se* is even more so, that is, more transitive. This is because critical thinking, as such, is a kind of higher-order thinking about things (e.g., problems, solutions, and questions) and is, therefore, parasitic upon the original thing being thought about. A person might, for example, be thinking about something but might yet not be in a position to think critically about that something. This is because critical thinking, as such, requires more than a minimal amount of understanding of that which is thought about. It is the consideration which leads me to hold that "critical thinking" is specific to the kind of thing being thought about. And insofar as there are logically different kinds of things to think about (e.g., problems and questions), it follows that there are logically different kinds of critical thinking. Hence, I oppose *general* critical thinking courses, which are supposed to be about everything in general and nothing in particular. I see nothing particularly "bizarre" in this rejection—quite the contrary.

The second argument Paul marshals to support his charge of "atomism" centers around the "multicategorical" character of most *real* problems. Paul argues that because I hold rationality and critical thinking to be domain- or subject-specific (i.e., atomistic, or specialist, he calls it), I therefore cannot handle most real, or "everyday" problems, because such problems do not lie clearly in one domain or another, but in several at once. They are "multicategorical." This is what I take to be the general thrust of his argument.

Let me say straightaway that I agree that *most* (but not all) real problems do lie in several domains at once, and are multitextured and multicategorical. I have no problems with this observation, and have been at pains to point it out myself in numerous places. What has gone wrong in Paul's argument is, again, to misinterpret my view regarding *how* domain-specific knowledge and understanding *function* to help us solve real problems. One of the reasons that I have been such a strong advocate of liberal education to develop critical thinking capacity is because I believe such an education helps to anticipate the multicategorical nature of most problems. A person needs several different kinds of knowledge and understanding to appreciate the different dimensions of most real problems. Real problems are indeed multifaceted and complex, and this is why no single set of skills, or clump of specific knowledge, can resolve them adequately.

When I talk about "domains of knowledge," it should be understood that I have something quite broad in mind. They are very close to Paul Hirst's notion of a "form of knowledge" or "form of rational discourse." (All of these notions originate in what Wittgenstein refers to as different "language games.") A liberal education enables a person to understand the different characteristics, procedures, "rules," and concepts which make up these broad "domains of rational discourse": and these are what one brings to bear on everyday problems. Metaphorically, we might think of a rational agent coping with the world in a similar way as the marine crab (i.e., the crustacean) copes with its aquatic environment. A crab is a single organism, yet it is composed of several different kinds of limbs, each designed to do a specific kind of job. It has pincers for holding things, antennae for navigating and checking things out, as well as several different pairs of legs, some of which are for balance, some for digging, and others for propulsion. Each specific kind of limb plays its role in enabling the crab to cope with its world. And more often than not (though not always), it uses several of its different kinds of limbs to cope with a single problem: each limb does its specific bit.

Similarly, rational human beings possess several logically distinct kinds of knowledge/understanding. And each kind (or kinds) of knowledge plays its particular role in solving particular problems. Should one of these domains be missing in a person (like a crab limb), or even underdeveloped, we might consider the person seriously deficient—as a crab without pincers, say. Liberal education tries to develop overall rationality by teaching people to understand, and to use, the different forms of rational discourse (e.g., math, science, morality, art, philosophy, etc.). Each form of knowledge provides a different kind of understanding and, therefore, can do different kinds of jobs (like different crab limbs.) None of this suggests, however, that problems fall neatly into one domain of understanding or another, or that only one domain is required to solve any problem.

What determines which domains of understanding will be required for any given problem depends, of course, on what the problem is, and what precisely you want answered. Consider, for a moment, Paul's counter example to my thesis. He says:

> Most of what we say and think, to put it another way, is not only open—but multitextured as well. For example, in what logical domain does the (technical?) concept of alcoholism solely belong: disease, addiction, crime, moral failing, cultural pattern, life-style choice, defect of socialization, self-comforting behavior, psychological escape, personal weakness . . . ? How many points of view can be used to illuminate it? Then, are each of them *in* one or many categories?

My answer to all of these questions is that it depends on what, precisely, you want to know or say about alcoholism. If one is interested in how widespread it is, or in which age-group, then it is a sociological question. If one wants to know if it is *right* or *wrong,* then it is a moral question. If one wants to know *why* people become alcoholics, then it is a psychological question. If one wants to know whether it is sinful, then I suppose this is a religious question. Many different *kinds* of things can be said and done with respect to alcoholism. It is simply one of those many things which do not belong to one and only one category. But as soon as one raises a specific kind of question about it, then a specific kind of answer will be appropriate; and one will have to draw upon the specific knowledge and understanding they have about that kind of question. Moreover, one kind of knowledge about things (like alcoholism) can often affect other beliefs one has about it as well. For example, if you believed alcoholism to be a disease, then you might not view it as a sin. But all of these cross-influences, and multitexturedness, does not gainsay the existence of categories through which we perceive, talk and think about things. Indeed, rational belief and action is often predicted on seeing things from these different perspectives; and people are not born with these different perspectives; they must learn them. Again, this is what a liberal education attempts to provide.

While some concepts, then, fall into several categories, there are also important concepts which are specific (or unique) to certain domains. For example, the notion of "moral obligations" belongs to ethics, just as "electromagnetism" belongs to physics, and "chiaroscuro" to art, "deity" to religion, "essence" and "ontology" to philosophy, and "differential equation" to mathematics, etc. Thus, some problems and questions we might have are peculiar to specific domains and, therefore, require knowledge of these domains in order to say anything intelligent about them. Of course, one can have varying degrees of such knowledge. Thus, one might be able to say and do some things within the domain but not others. One's abilities here are a function of one's knowledge in the domain.[1]

Moreover, I want to stress two further points about this domain-specific knowledge. First, it is not simply esoteric or useless knowledge designed to serve the interests of academic specialists, but rather, *education,* as such, consists in introducing people to the fundamentals of this knowledge in order to increase their rational capacities. Second, very many (if not most) so-called everyday problems need to employ domain-specific knowledge of this sort, if the discussion is to move beyond a superficial level. Indeed, this is why the more persistent "everyday problems" such as disarmament, pollution, pornography, etc., are not amenable to quick solutions. They require several different *kinds* of specific knowledge and judgment, and sometimes in considerable amount. A broad liberal education is simply the best that we can do to bring average citizens up to the task of making rational judgments about such problems. And even this, perforce, will be incomplete and fallible. But it is likely to be our best bet. Considerations such as these are what prompted my comment that "in this age of increased special knowledge, there are few Renaissance men." It was not meant to suggest that all problems fall neatly into one specialist's domain or another, as Paul interprets it.

Two brief (and final) points about Paul's charge of "atomism" and knowledge domains. First, there have been thirteen published reviews of my book to date, and Richard Paul's is the first to construe my view as *specialistic* (or atomistic). It has been quite clear to most readers that I call for a broad liberal education, and that this is not "atomistic." I think, therefore, that his misinterpretation of my position is more Paul's own doing than it is mine. Second, Paul states in several places that a person's worldview, or knowledge *überhaupt,* plays a crucial role in their critical thinking capacities. I could not agree more strongly. However, if Paul would take the time to examine seriously the ingredients of a person's "worldview," I think he would find it composed of certain kinds of beliefs and knowledge structures (i.e., cognitive schemata), which is precisely what liberal education attempts to influence and enlighten. Thus, there is actually more agreement here than Paul seems comfortable to admit. I just don't think his continued use of the phrase *worldview* adds anything different to what we are already familiar with—but I have no objection to the phrase.

Enough about the *major* philosophical differences between Paul's view and my own. There remains one niggling point which I will briefly comment upon here only because Paul devotes so much space to it, and I might seem remiss if I omitted it.

In the middle of Paul's review, he charges me with presenting critiques of the work of Scriven, D'Angelo, Ennis, and Johnson and Blair which are "unfair," "unsympathetic," and "at times highly misleading." Clearly, I cannot go over all of this ground again without writing another book. But a few comments, at least, are in order. First, if I have been "unfair" to any of these writers, I hereby apologize for it. They may rest assured that any unfairness was unintentional. One does one's best. I might say, however, that I have had lengthy contact with both Scriven and D'Angelo since the book was published, and neither of them ever suggested that my treatment of them was unfair. Indeed, despite remaining differences over more technical matters, they have both thanked me for much of my critique. Johnson and Blair strongly disagree with my views about informal logic, but they have never written (nor said) that I was unfair, nor seriously misrepresented their views.

Ennis, apparently, does think that I have been unfair to his view. But disagreement, which there is, does not amount to unfairness or "misleading representation," as Paul charges. Ennis's so-called range definition remains an *attempt* at definition, nonetheless; and one which I find deficient for all the reasons I provided. Its core ingredient consists in a list of "general reasoning skills" which I reject. Moreover, Ennis still clings to the idea that "general reasoning skills" should be taught in order to improve critical thinking. He reiterates this point again and again in several recent publications. I think he is wrong about this for all the reasons I have given in the book, here, and elsewhere. This disagreement is not "misrepresentation," but a *bona fide* difference of opinion.

With respect to Ennis leaving out any treatment of value judgments and making that clear to his reader, I specifically discuss this point on page 54 of my book. Indeed, I explicitly quote Ennis's own words explaining why he left it out; moreover, it does not appear in a footnote somewhere, but in the middle of the text itself. So there is no attempt at "misrepresentation" here. I then go on to point out that it is a serious omission because his "pragmatic dimension" of critical thinking necessarily requires making value judgments. I still think this is correct. But even if Paul (or perhaps Ennis) disagrees with this observation, it is *not* misrepresentation.

To conclude, I want to address two relatively minor, but interesting, comments of Paul's. The first comment appears in his final, lengthy footnote. Here, Paul questions and criticizes the appropriateness of a book on critical thinking devoting an entire chapter to Edward de Bono's work on thinking. Paul makes several points: (1) de Bono does not explicitly treat *critical* thinking as most of us understand the phrase (rather, he treats "problem solving" and "creativity" more than anything else); (2) de Bono is not in the same theoretical league as Scriven, Ennis, *et al.*; and (3) perhaps de Bono was only included in my book for his "celebrity." I must remind Richard Paul (and possibly the reader) that I consider myself a philosopher of education, and I write from that perspective. Indeed, the title of my monograph is *Critical Thinking and Education*. Thus, whatever Richard Paul's particular theoretical pretenses, it just happens to be the case that de Bono's thinking programs are widely used in schools throughout the world and, therefore, have direct educational relevance. Moreover, these programs are very commonly used in many schools as *bona fide* critical thinking programs. Thus, first, if I had *not* treated de Bono at some length, educators (the major audience) would have found the omission indeed very strange; and, second, my purpose was to expose the inherent weaknesses in de Bono's programs for educators and philosophers alike. I still believe this needed to be done for educators, and this is the kind of contribution that philosophers of education often make. Interestingly, I have received several letters from philosophers of education in Great Britain, where de Bono's programs are widely used, who were greatly appreciative of that chapter in particular. (Antony Flew also has commented to this effect in the *Times Educational Supplement,* 29 January 1982.) These, then, were the reasons for treating de Bono's work at some length. And finally, it remains a mystery to me why Richard Paul, given his reservation about de Bono's status, invited him to speak at his annual Sonoma conference on thinking, though I am happy that he did so.

The second minor point to be treated here relates, similarly, to Paul's apparent ignorance about developments in the field of philosophy of education proper. Paul quotes a statement of mine about *education* and *schooling* that he apparently finds so cockeyed that it doesn't even warrant a counterargument by him. He just confidently states that his reader will not be "comfortable" with it either. He quotes me saying that "there is nothing in the logic of 'education' that requires that schools should engage in education" and "nothing contradictory in saying, 'This is a fine school, and I recommend it to others, even though it does not engage in education.' " To Paul, such a locution sounds patently absurd; to me, it is almost trivially true. This conflict of opinion is a dramatic example of something which Harvey Siegel has drawn to people's attention in several recent papers; namely, that it "is high time that the Informal Logic Movement confront the philosophy of education."[2] It is quite clear to Siegel, and to me, that the ILM continues to proceed along its high-profile path without the slightest knowledge of the more serious literature in the philosophy of education. Anyone who had read R. S. Peters, Paul Hirst, or Robert Dearden, or a number of contemporary American philosophers of education would immediately understand that "schooling" and "education" are conceptually different things, and neither one entails the other. There are ballet schools, barber schools, flight schools, and numerous other kinds of schools whose purpose is not *education* in the normal (or traditional) sense, but rather *training* of some kind. A highly trained barber may or may not be educated. In short, some schools are avowedly *not* in the business of producing "educated people." They are teaching something else, e.g., different job skills, etc. The purpose of schools in many third world countries is to teach improved agricultural skills, road building, hygiene, and the like, perhaps so that they might eventually have the luxury of *educating* their populations in the more traditional sense. What schools are *for* is a social decision which varies from place to place, and sometimes from school to school. Thus, there is nothing particularly strange, nor contradictory, in my saying that "there is nothing in the logic of 'education' that requires that schools should engage in 'education.' " Much goes on in schools which has nothing to do with "education" as such; and, conversely, much "education" (e.g., self-education) does not take place in schools. Philosophers of education know this.

Notes

Chapter 1

1. To those tempted to maintain that the phrase "general reasoning ability" is at least *coherent*, possibly on the grounds that it remains a perfectly good English phrase, I would argue that: (1) it is so systematically vague that it fails to discriminate any particular cognitive function; and (2) it does not denote any particular skill nor any enumerable set of skills.

2. For documentation and further discussion of this point, see my *Critical Thinking and Education*, Oxford, Martin Robertson, 1981, p. 85.

3. For example, an assumption of the proposition "Some of us will go home in automobiles" might be that many of us arrived here that way. This *assumption* could in fact be false (e.g., if we took a bus, walked, or biked) yet the proposition is still true. But if the *presupposition* that some of us do in fact go home is false, then the proposition cannot be true.

4. There are also significant psychological and/or emotive difficulties associated with getting students to be self-critical about their own beliefs and prejudices. However, I am here restricting myself to considerations which fall more directly into the *cognitive* domain (in contrast to the *affective* domain).

5. Scriven's "principles" are different, but his general strategy is the same.

6. Among them, Scriven's *Applied Logic: An Introduction to Scientific Reasoning*, Palo Alto, Calif., Behavioral Research Laboratories, 1966; and "Education for Survival," 1972. In *Curriculum and the Cultural Revolution*, (eds.) D. E. Pupel & M. Belanger (McCutchon: Berkeley, Calif.)

Chapter 2

1. I use the phrase "true critical thinking" here, not to beg the question, but to rule out those few authors who almost *define* critical thinking in terms of possessing certain preferred skills (e.g., those who use "informal logic skills" as synonymous with "critical thinking"). This move does beg the question.

2. J. J. Schwab, "Structures of the Disciplines: Meanings and Slogans." Quoted from I. A. Snook, "The Concept of Indoctrination," *Studies in Philosophy of Education* 7:2 (Fall 1970).

Chapter 3

1. For an interesting and important discussion of the issues surrounding this entire thesis, see John C. Bishop, "Can There Be Thought without Language?" in *Thinking: The Expanding Frontier,* Philadelphia, Franklin Institute Press, 1983, pp. 13–23.

2. Incidentally, if you consider Jerome Bruner's sage advice, I think you will see that his notion of the "structure of a discipline," such as that found in MACOS, is primarily an attempt to have children understand "disciplinary thinking," first and foremost.

3. For a rich and critical discussion of this distinction as found in the work of B. Bloom, G. Ryle, P. Geach, and Jane Rolland Martin, see James Gribble, *Introduction to Philosophy of Education,* (Boston, Allyn and Bacon, 1969), pp. 59–70.

Chapter 4

1. All of this, incidentally, is also compatible with Paul Hirst's notion of the "forms of knowledge." While I prefer to regard the "forms" as forms of *rational discourse* (and not "knowledge," as such), my thinking has been greatly influenced by Hirst.

2. Most of these studies are cited and reported upon in Robert Glaser's "Education and Thinking: The Role of Knowledge," *American Psychologist,* Feb. 1984.

3. Quoted from ibid., p. 104.

4. This literature is to be found within the field of "curriculum theory" in education. A good place to begin is J. Bruner's *Process of Education,* New York, Vintage Books, 1960; G. W. Ford and F. Pugno, *The Structure of Knowledge and the Curriculum,* Chicago, Rand McNally, 1964. Also, the curriculum work of Northrop Frye for literature, and of Elliot Eisner for art education, are strong on the notion of teaching structures.

Chapter 5

1. See my *Critical Thinking and Education,* Oxford, Martin Robertson, 1981.

2. See, in particular, Robert Ennis, "Logic and Critical Thinking," *Proceedings of the Philosophy of Education Society* 1981: 228–32.

3. Ibid., pp. 229 and 231.

4. For a representative sample of this literature, see David and Linda Annis, "Does Philosophy Improve Critical Thinking?" *Teaching Philosophy* 3:2 (Fall 1979); Daryl G. Smith, "College Classroom Interaction and Critical Thinking," *Journal of Educational Psychology* 69 (1977): 180; Bruce L. Stewart, *Testing for Critical Thinking: A Review of the Resources,* Illinois Rational Thinking Project, Report 2, Urbana, Ill., Bureau of Educational Research, 1979; Thomas N. Tomko and Robert H. Ennis, "Evaluation of Informal Logic Competence," J. A. Blair and R. H. Johnson, eds., *Infor-*

mal Logic: The First International Symposium (1980): Edgepress: Pt. Reyes, CA.

5. Originally printed in *Psychological Review* 1956.

6. *The Psychology of Deductive Reasoning*, London, Routledge and Kegan Paul, 1982, pp. 6 and 254.

7. David P. Ausubel, *Educational Psychology: A Cognitive View*, 2d ed., New York, Holt, Rinehart, 1978 p. 544.

8. "The Teaching of Thinking" first appeared in *The School Review* 73 (1965): 1–13; reprinted and quoted here from J. P. Shaver and H. Berlak, eds., *Democracy, Pluralism and the Social Studies*, Boston, Houghton Mifflin, 1968, pp. 384–92.

9. Dressel and Mayhew are quoted by Watson-Glaser in their manual: The Manual for *Watson-Glaser Critical Thinking Appraisal*, New York, Harcourt Brace Jovanovich, 1980, p. 1.

10. Op. cit., p. 231.

11. *Teaching Philosophy* 3:2 (Fall 1979): 145–52.

12. "On the Uses of Educational Connoisseurship and Criticism for Evaluating Classroom Life," *Teacher College Record* 78:3 (Feb. 1977): 349.

13. Op. cit., pp. 145 and 148.

14. For criticisms of this test, see Stewart, *Testing for Critical Thinking: A Review of the Resources;* see also my *Critical Thinking and Education*.

Chapter 6

1. G. Ryle, *The Concept of Mind*, New York, Barnes and Noble, 1949.

2. R. S. Peters, *The Concept of Motivation*, London, Routledge and Kegan Paul, 1958.

3. R. H. Ennis, "A Conception of Rational Thinking," in J. R. Coombs, ed., *Philosophy of Education 1979*, Normal, Ill., The Philosophy of Education Society, 1980, pp. 3–30.

4. I. Scheffler, *The Language of Education*, Springfield, Ill., Charles C. Thomas, 1960, pp. 19–22.

5. D. Hitchcock, *Critical Thinking: A Guide to Evaluating Information*, Toronto, Methuen, 1983, pp. 145–46.

6. R. H. Ennis, "A Conception of Deductive Logical Competence," *Teaching Philosophy* 4 (1981): 337–85.

7. J. E. McPeck, *Critical Thinking and Education*, Oxford: Martin Robertson, 1981, p. 39.

8. S. P. Norris, "Competence as Powers," in E. E. Robertson, ed., *Philosophy of Education 1984*, Normal, Ill.; The Philosophy of Education Society, 1985.

9. S. P. Norris, "The Choice of Standard Conditions in Defining Critical Thinking Competence," *Educational Theory 35* (1985): 97–107.

10. See Ennis, "A Conception of Deductive Logical Competence."

11. J. St. B. T. Evans, *The Psychology of Deductive Reasoning,* London: Routledge and Kegan Paul, 1982.

12. McPeck, op. cit., p. 185.

13. Ibid., p. 56

14. See Evans, op. cit.

15. G. Watson and E. M. Glaser, *Watson-Glaser Critical Thinking Appraisal, Form A,* New York: The Psychological Corporation, 1980.

16. R. H. Ennis, "Problems in Testing Informal Logic Critical Thinking Reasoning Ability," *Informal Logic* 6:1 (1984): 3–9.

17. R. H. Ennis and J. Millman, *Cornell Critical Thinking Test, Level Z,* Champaign, Ill.; Illinois Rational Thinking Project, 1982.

18. McPeck, op. cit., p. 146.

19. Ennis, op. cit., p. 9, n. 3.

20. S. P. Norris and R. King, *The Design of a Critical Thinking Test on Appraising Observations,* St. John's, Newfoundland, Institute for Educational Research and Development, Memorial University of Newfoundland, 1984.

Chapter 7

1. As Richard Paul puts it, ILM "ought to move to become the professional group that superintends the teaching of logic-critical thinking skills in public schools and so universalize its influence in education" ("An Agenda Item for the Informal Logic/Critical Thinking Movement," *Informal Logic Newsletter* 5 [1983]: 24). Similarly, J. A. Blair and R. H. Johnson offer as one of the attitudes which characterize ILM the following: "An orientation that treats the teaching of reasoning skills as a key part of education, integral . . . to preparation of youth for responsible social and political roles," (Introduction to *Informal Logic: The First International Symposium,* Inverness, Calif., Edgepress, 1980, p. x).
   As Blair has forcefully pointed out to me, it is misleading to speak of the ILM as a monolithic group with universally shared viewpoints. On the contrary, philosophers who identify themselves with the ILM differ widely on virtually every matter of group interest. Indeed, the very identification of the ILM and its members is problematic. Roughly, I have in mind those persons who read *Informal Logic;* belong to the Association for Informal Logic and Critical Thinking (AILACT), which is affiliated with the American Philosophical Association; attend conferences on critical thinking and/ or informal logic held periodically at the University of Windsor, Sonoma State University, and elsewhere; and teach courses in informal logic and/ or critical thinking. The diversity of opinion among such a wide collection of persons is—I agree with Blair—very great. Nevertheless, some generalizations, such as the ones which appear in this paragraph, seem to me appropriate.

2. John McPeck, *Critical Thinking and Education,* Oxford, Martin Robertson, 1981. In subsequent references to this book, emphases are in the original unless otherwise noted.

3. Ibid., p. 3.

4. Ibid., p. 5.

5. Ibid., p. 4.

6. Cf. Richard Paul's similar criticism in his review of McPeck's book, in *Educational Leadership* (forthcoming), Stephen P. Norris's excellent discussion of this issue in "The Choice of Standard Conditions in Defining Critical Thinking Competence," *Educational Theory* 35 (1985): 97–107, and Perry Weddle's review of McPeck's book in *Informal Logic* 6 (1984): 23–25.

7. McPeck, op. cit., p. 6.

8. Ibid., p. 7.

9. Ibid., pp. 7–8.

10. Ibid., p. 8.

11. Ibid.

12. Ibid., p. 9.

13. Ibid.

14. Ibid., p. 13.

15. Further discussion of this conception of critical thinking may be found in my "Critical Thinking as an Educational Ideal," *The Educational Forum* 45 (1980): 7–23; and my "Educational Ideals and Educational Practice: The Case of Minimum Competency Testing," *Issues in Education* 1 (1984): 154–70. Robert W. Binkley also holds something like this two-part conception of critical thinking/good reasoning; see his "Can the Ability to Reason Well Be Taught?" in *Informal Logic,* pp. 79–92.

16. McPeck, op. cit., p. 19.

17. Ibid., p. 22.

18. Ibid.

19. Ibid., p. 23.

20. In the paper mentioned in the footnote at the beginning of this chapter, I argue that the development of an epistemological account of reasons, and of the relation A bears to B when A is a reason for B, is one of the central philosophical tasks to which the ILM must address itself. The above discussion of formal logic is taken largely from my "Educational Ideals and Educational Practice: The Case of Minimum Competency Testing."

21. The two distinctions McPeck draws are closely related: logic is to be distinguished from critical thinking precisely because it is not logic, but information, which is relevant to reason assessment. They are of a piece. Nevertheless, it serves clarification more fully to separate the distinctions and discuss each in turn.

22. McPeck, op. cit., p. 23.

23. Ibid., p. 28.

24. Ibid., p. 56.

25. Ibid., p. 64.

26. Ibid., pp. 23–24.

27. Ibid., p. 12.

28. Israel Scheffler, *Conditions of Knowledge,* Chicago, Scott, Foresman, 1965, p. 107. Further discussion of Scheffler and of the relation between critical thinking and rationality is my "Critical Thinking as an Educational Ideal."

29. Larry Laudan, *Progress and Its Problems,* Berkeley, University of California Press, 1977, p. 123. Critical discussion of Laudan's application of this point to the problem of the rationality of science may be found in my "Truth, Problem Solving and the Rationality of Science," *Studies in History and Philosophy of Science* 14 (1983): 89–112.

30. I take them up in the papers mentioned in the footnote at the beginning of this chapter.

Chapter 9

1. In addition, there is a growing number of national and international conferences on the subject, for example, the First and Second International Symposia on Informal Logic, the First and Second National Conferences on Critical Thinking, Moral Education, and Rationality; and the First International Conference on Critical Thinking, Education, and the Rational Person.

2. J. A. Blair and R. H. Johnson, eds., *Informal Logic: The Proceedings of the First International Conference on Informal Logic,* Pt. Reyes, Calif., Edgepress, 1980.

3. Such a course is now a graduation requirement for all California state college and university system students, as well as for the California community college system.

4. Robert Ennis, "A Concept of Critical Thinking," *Harvard Educational Review* 1962.

5. Something should be said in passing about McPeck's treatment of Edward de Bono, to whose ideas he devotes a full chapter. This is odd, given the book's supposed focus on critical thinking, for de Bono has no theory of critical thinking as such, unless his stereotype of critical thinking as uncreative fault finding qualifies as such. Indeed, de Bono uses the concept of critical thinking merely as a foil for "lateral" or "creative" thinking, which he of course takes to be essentially different. He holds that we already put too great an emphasis on *critical* thought. Perhaps McPeck includes him because of his celebrity. I find this inclusion inappropriate and the amount of attention devoted to him unjustified, if critical thinking is indeed McPeck's concern. Furthermore, de Bono is clearly not in the same league theoretically as an Ennis, D'Angelo, or Scriven, whatever his

celebrity, and his kaleidoscopic, helter-skelter development of metaphors, which merely suggest rather than theoretically probe the character of "lateral" thought, is an easy target for critique.

Chapter 10

1. An extensive review of recent psychological investigations into reasoning and reasoning skills has been published by Robert Glaser (University of Pittsburgh) in *The American Psychologist,* February 1984, entitled "Education and Thinking: The Role of Knowledge." This paper points out that most of the responsible research in this field strongly supports the view that domain-specific knowledge is the major determinant of reasoning skill. Even artificial intelligence (AI) research is making stronger progress since it has turned away from a "general strategies approach" and toward a "knowledge-based approach." (See also M. Minsky and S. Papert, *Artificial Intelligence,* Eugene, Ore., Oregon State System of Higher Education, 1974). Much rhetoric to the contrary, defenders of generalized reasoning skills (e.g., the ILM) are defending a rear-guard action and not a new breakthrough.

2. See his "Educating Reason: Critical Thinking, Informal Logic and the Philosophy of Education" in the *ATA Newsletter on Teaching Philosophy,* Special Issue on Informal Logic and Critical Thinking, Spring–Summer 1985, p. 10.

Index